DE GRUYTER

IAN GRAY
JOHN BESSANT

THE SCALING VALUE PLAYBOOK

A practical guide for creating innovation networks for impact and growth

TABLE OF CONTENTS

 **DOWNLOAD**

Worksheets marked with this icon can be downloaded here:

▷ www.degruyter.com/document/isbn/9783110789812/html

▷ www.scalingvalue.org/toolkit

PART 1
PREPARING FOR THE SCALING EXPEDITION

CHAPTER I	WHAT'S THE PROBLEM?	8
CHAPTER II	MAPPING THE JOURNEY TO SCALE	28
CHAPTER III	MANAGING THE SCALE EXPEDITION: THE POWER OF VALUE NETWORKS	58
CHAPTER IV	CONFIGURING VALUE NETWORKS	66
CHAPTER V	WORKING WITH VALUE ROLES: MANAGING OUR NETWORK	90
CHAPTER VI	SCALE STORIES	102

PART 2
WORKING ON YOUR JOURNEY TO SCALE

CHAPTER VII	BASE CAMP VISIONING: WHERE ARE WE GOING?	142
CHAPTER VIII	SOLUTION	154
CHAPTER IX	ORGANISATION	174
CHAPTER X	BOOKENDS	184
CHAPTER XI	MOVERS	196
CHAPTER XII	SHAPERS	206
CHAPTER XIII	DEVELOPING VALUE NETWORKS	214
CHAPTER XIV	SCALE STRATEGY	228

AFTERWORD

Looking across the range	235
Further resources	236
Acknowledgements	238
About the authors	240

PART 1

PREPARING FOR THE SCALING EXPEDITION

CHAPTER I
WHAT'S THE PROBLEM? ———— 8

CHAPTER II
MAPPING THE JOURNEY TO SCALE ———— 28

CHAPTER III
MANAGING THE SCALE EXPEDITION:
THE POWER OF VALUE NETWORKS ———— 58

CHAPTER IV
CONFIGURING VALUE NETWORKS ———— 66

CHAPTER V
WORKING WITH VALUE ROLES:
MANAGING OUR NETWORK ———— 90

CHAPTER VI
SCALE STORIES ———— 102

PART 1   PREPARING FOR THE SCALING EXPEDITION

CHAP

WHAT'S THE PROBLEM?

Innovation is hard enough just to get from idea to launch. But launching your innovation and having small-scale success is only half the journey. Creating real impact requires a different approach, and it's hard even for experienced players. This chapter explores what we've learned about the scale expedition and how the book will help you think about, plan and carry yours through.

THE INNOVATION MOUNTAIN BASE CAMP: A SERIES OF PILOTS

» Many technologists believe that advantageous innovations will sell themselves, that the obvious benefits of a new idea will be widely realised by potential adopters, and that the innovation will diffuse rapidly. Seldom is this the case. «

EVERETT ROGERS
Diffusion of innovations

INNOVATION ISN'T EASY

Mr. James Murray Spangler had a chequered life with plenty of ups and downs. An inveterate inventor, he'd had some success with his ideas for things like a grain harvester, a winnowing rake and a velocipede wagon – a form of bicycle-powered cart. But in 1907 he was down on his luck, sweeping up after hours as a janitor in Zollinger's department store in Ohio. Not the best job for someone with a bad chest; he coughed

SWEEPING THE FLOOR WITH INNOVATION

You can find a longer version of the Spangler story which describes the challenges in moving great innovation ideas to scale by following this link.

and spluttered in the dust which swirled around his brushes. But that led him to a classic piece of user innovation: he cobbled together a strange looking device, which was eventually patented as the ⏭ 'ELECTRIC VACUUM SUCTION SWEEPER'.

Convinced of its utility, he borrowed money, set up a small factory and began selling door-to-door. But his great idea failed to scale fast enough; he was falling deeper and deeper into debt. Fortunately, he'd given one of his precious cleaners to his cousin who was delighted with it, so much so that she explained its virtues to her husband. This turned out to be a very good thing for Mr. Spangler because the husband in question was William Hoover, a successful businessman. He decided to buy the patent (and hire Mr. Spangler) and set the vacuum cleaner business on a more secure footing. It wasn't an overnight success – it took a lot of hard work and Hoover's many connections, but finally it took off. This is why today you'll often hear people talk about 'hoovering' the floor rather than 'spanglering' it.

Spangler isn't alone – there are plenty of others who were successful but fell at this scaling fence. Consider Elias Howe, the man who first patented the sewing machine but failed to build a business around his idea; it was left to Isaac Singer to grow the business (and add his name).

It's a continuing problem. Think of the revolution in portable entertainment which has led to the smartphone experience we have today. The world's first portable MP3 player was the MPMan F10, manufactured by South Korea's SaeHan Information Systems and launched in March 1998. It worked well at a technical level: with its 32MB of memory you could carry a handful of your favourite songs around with you and change your playlist by hooking up to your computer. It didn't exactly set the world on fire and a price tag of $250 made it very much a niche product.

It was followed by a variety of look-alikes, all launched by entrepreneurs spotting the huge potential market opportunity, but it was a relative latecomer to the game which cleaned up. Apple's iPod launched in 2001 and, although it had an iconic design, it was the smooth interface to a huge library of legal downloads via iTunes that finally moved the product into the mainstream of must-have consumer electronics

CHAP WHAT'S THE PROBLEM?

DUPONT

DuPont is a 200-year-old company with a long history in chemicals. Originally founded by a French emigrant their early products included gunpowder, but they quickly diversified into the exploding field of industrial chemicals. They pioneered the manufacture of synthetic textiles and plastics and continue to play an important role in the industry.

The better mousetrap that no one wants

Sometimes the problem is that you have a great – and ➜ PROVEN – INNOVATION, it's just that the world remains stubbornly unconvinced. *Earl Tupper* was a smart and successful entrepreneur. Having tried several times to start his own businesses (failing each time but learning and reapplying himself), he spent several years with ○ DUPONT learning the newly emerging technology of plastics. He left them to set up on his own company and built a successful business during the war years.

By the late 1940s he was playing with a number of new product ideas. His big breakthrough came with the almost alchemical idea of turning the by-product black sludge from oil wells into a colourful range of lightweight plastic storage containers. He topped off his idea with a patented seal, borrowing from the paint industry the mechanism through which they ensured that paint didn't spill out of cans. His launch of Tupperware was well received by early enthusiasts, and the buyers at big department stores saw it as the perfect product with which to brighten their kitchenware shelves. A feature in the influential *House Beautiful* magazine even called the Tupperware range "fine art for 39 cents."

➜ **PROVEN INNOVATION**

Something which has gone beyond being a 'value proposition' – a nice idea which might be of interest – to an actual solution which has been developed and sold and which, at least on a small scale, is successful.

THE TUPPERWARE STORY

Yet this wonderful innovation, successfully prototyped and launched – and with proven advantages – stubbornly refused to sell. It was only when Tupper encountered a single mother, Brownie Wise, that things began to turn around. She was a natural saleswoman but was particularly successful in pioneering a new approach, first with the Stanley Home Products company and then branching out on her own with her company Patio Parties. The model was simple: instead of selling door-to-door, she hosted parties in people's homes, and instead of using sales representatives, she got the women who hosted the parties to be part of the sales force. Wise pioneered the idea of what we now term 'social marketing', developing the channels and influencers to ensure adoption right around the world at scale. Tupper took her on to run the sales side of his business – and the rest, as they say, is history. Today's Tupperware can be found throughout the world and has annual sales in excess of $1 billion.

 Otto Rohwedder had a similar problem: like Tupper he'd come up with a great idea and worked hard to bring it to life. A gifted inventor, he had developed a machine for producing sliced bread. Its journey from idea to innovation was a long and arduous one; along the way his factory burnt down and he nearly went bankrupt in 1917. But 10 years later he was able to file a patent and set up the Mac-Roh Company to launch his great idea, only to see it arrive with more of a whimper than a bang. The bakers to whom he tried to sell it were underwhelmed. They thought the machine too complex for everyday production: it was bulky and took up precious space – and they weren't convinced of the need anyway. Teetering once again on the edge of bankruptcy, he persuaded a local baker, Frank Bench, to invest and install the first machine.

On July 7, 1928, the first loaf of commercially sliced bread was produced by the Chillicothe Baking Company of Missouri and sold under the brand name Kleen Maid. And while bakers had been sceptical of the benefits, local families in the Midwest were much more enthusiastic: within two weeks bread sales from the bakery had increased by 2,000%! The idea began to take off across the country and two years later the New York-based Continental Baking Company began using Rohwedder's machines to build an entire business around sliced bread. Their product, Wonder Bread, and the accompanying marketing campaign helped lift awareness to a high level. By 1933, almost every bakery in the USA had

THE BEST THING SINCE SLICED BREAD?

What's the story behind sliced bread – and does it have any useful lessons for innovation managers today?

CHAP | WHAT'S THE PROBLEM? 13

a slicing machine and 80% of the bread produced in America was sliced.

It takes time

Sometimes it's all about change taking place at a glacially slow pace. Think about the innovation of → CASH PROGRAMMING, today one of the 'power tools' in the humanitarian and development toolbox. It has now become widely used, but the journey to scale for that idea took over 30 years and is still continuing. Or Muhammad Yunus's wonderful idea for →○ 'MICROFINANCE' – providing small loans to help fledgling entrepreneurs get started in local ventures. This revolution began in Bangladesh with the foundation of Grameen Bank in 1983. It took 10 years to make the short move to India, and a further 24 years before the innovation achieved real scale. By 2015, some 78 microfinance institutions with a combined gross portfolio of $1.4 billion were able to serve nearly 10 million active borrowers – but this journey to scale was a long and arduous one.

We can see a similarly long journey in the work of George Washington Carver, who spent his working lifetime trying to find ways to scale proven agricultural in-

MICROFINANCE

The idea of 'microfinance' is providing loan opportunities to people who would not normally be able to access the banking system. Typically, the amounts of money involved are small – less than $100 – but they can make a big difference to the lives of people on low incomes; the model has enabled many small-scale entrepreneurs to grow successful businesses.

→ **CASH PROGRAMMING**

In the world of humanitarian aid cash programming refers to the practice of giving people money to purchase food, medicines and other necessities instead of providing and distributing these items via aid agencies. For more on this see:

novations to the rural farming population in the USA. The challenge he faced was essentially one of 'crossing the chasm' – how to accelerate the adoption of proven successful innovations from a small group of early enthusiasts across to the ▷◁ MAINSTREAM.

It's no easier in the commercial world: the Toyota Prius revolutionised thinking (and sales) around 'green' vehicles, but it took over 10 years to reach economic scale. McDonald's is often put forward as an example of a scaling success, but as Ray Kroc (the architect of their scaling journey) once commented, "I was an overnight success all right, but 30 years is a long, long night."

Assembling the jigsaw

Sometimes the best ideas run aground in their implementation; the devil is not only in the detail, but is sometimes also in the challenge of having to bring many different elements together into a viable system. Israeli entrepreneur Shai Agassi was no shrinking violet – you only have to look at his famous 2009 🔗 TED talk to be convinced by his passion and vision for making the world a better place through electromobility. He also convinced a lot of influential people to come along

PODCAST

CASE STUDY

SHAI AGASSI

> MCDONALD'S IS OFTEN PUT FORWARD AS AN EXAMPLE OF A SCALING SUCCESS, BUT AS RAY KROC (THE ARCHITECT OF THEIR SCALING JOURNEY) ONCE COMMENTED, "I WAS AN OVERNIGHT SUCCESS ALL RIGHT, BUT 30 YEARS IS A LONG, LONG NIGHT."

with him: his Better Place venture raised a quarter of a billion dollars (for its time the fifth-largest start-up investment in business history) and support from the ex-prime minister of Israel and the CEO of Renault-Nissan to get behind its launch in 2011.

The idea was simple and compelling: eliminate one of the big obstacles to the adoption of electric vehicles (i.e., range anxiety) by using battery swap technology. Where you'd typically drive into a filling station for fuel, you'd similarly drive up to a swap station and in a few minutes your old depleted battery will have been replaced by a fully charged new one and you're good to go.

The technology worked; demonstrations of the swap stations brought the vision to life. But between the proven technology and its eventual diffusion lay a big chasm: getting all the elements of the system in place. Agassi was never able to implement his vision of a network of swap stations at sufficient scale for people to risk buying the cars and switching their behaviour. Better Place eventually went bankrupt in 2013 having racked up huge losses.

THE CHALLENGE OF SCALE

All these examples share the common theme that they are not about wacky inventions or front-end uncertainty. They are proven successful solutions. They just struggled to scale. It's a widespread problem – there's even a *Museum of Failure* dedicated to innovation might-have-beens and a good proportion of its exhibits are examples of failure to scale. Nor is it a small or inexperienced firm problem – big names like Toshiba (think about its $1 billion loss on trying and failing to bring HD DVD to scale) Coca-Cola (New Coke), Apple (the Newton) or Gerber (pureed convenience food for busy people – essentially baby food in a jar for adults) all remind us that making it to scale isn't an easy journey.

MUSEUM OF FAILURE

> **UNLIKE THE CARTOON PICTURES WHICH SUGGEST THAT THERE IS NOTHING TO IT, INNOVATION IS ACTUALLY AN EXTENDED JOURNEY MOVING FROM AN IDEA TO SOMETHING WHICH CREATES VALUE.**

Scaling as a journey

Innovation isn't about light-bulb moments. Unlike the cartoon pictures which suggest that there is nothing to it, innovation is actually an extended journey moving from an idea to something which creates value. That journey is not without its twists and turns; it's roadblocks and one-way streets which require detours, but there is a pattern to it which by now is fairly well understood. It involves a series of stages, moving from search and ideation, finding promising ideas, through to selecting the best and then implementing them. That process involves considerable iteration and pivoting, but eventually a solution emerges which can be launched and piloted.

We understand a lot about the front end of this process – to the point where there is extensive guidance available to help would-be innovators get as far as launching and piloting. But we're only halfway along our innovation journey at this point; ahead of us is the extended part of the journey through highly uncertain territory towards scale. And there remains a lot less information around how we might manage or support that journey to scale.

WHAT'S THE PROBLEM?

SUCCESS STORIES: IT CAN BE DONE
Of course it's not all bad news; there are plenty of examples of innovations which have successfully scaled. Think about the following examples.

1 **Ray Kroc's vision was that there would be 1,000 McDonald's restaurants solely in the United States.** Yet, McDonald's continued to grow and expand into international markets beginning in 1967 by opening in Canada and Puerto Rico. In 2022 the company had a turnover close to $6 billion in sales from over 36,000 restaurants in over 100 nations.

2 **Malcolm McLean had an idea while sitting on the dockside back in 1956 of developing a simpler system for loading, unloading and transporting goods:** the humble shipping container. Within a couple of years he had transformed the process, cutting costly waiting times for ships and accelerating trade as a result. Today there are around 23 million containers [1] in transit somewhere around the world and the era of globalisation has been enabled by his innovation.

3 **Jeff Bezos of Amazon picked up an idea originally pioneered by Aaron Montgomery Ward in 1872 and successfully brought to scale by Richard Warren Sears and Alvah Roebuck in 1887 [2] with their catalogue business.** Using the new medium of the internet he reframed bookselling and then diversified into remote retailing across an increasing number of sectors, establishing a platform and supporting infrastructure to enable others to transact all kinds of business across it. Today Amazon is one of the largest companies in the world with a huge global reach.

4 **Dr. Govindappa Venkataswamy retired after a long and successful career as an eye surgeon in southern India to follow his passion for improving eye care amongst the poor in that country.** He established a small 11-bed facility in 1976 and deployed a radically different approach to the problem, drawing on experiences from far outside the health sector in the worlds of fast food and car manufacturing. His Aravind Eye Care System [3] now treats hundreds of thousands of patients each year and has been responsible for restoring sight to over 20 million people. The model has been widely emulated and adapted for other forms of healthcare around the world.

5 **M-PESA means 'mobile money' in Swahili and is a system for cash transfer operated over mobile phones.** Originally a development aid project sponsored by the UK's Department for International Development partnering with Safaricom (part of the Vodafone group), M-PESA [4] transactions now account for over 50% of GDP in Kenya [5] and the model has been widely applied elsewhere as an alternative to conventional banking systems.

1 www.budgetshippingcontainers.co.uk/info/how-many-shipping-containers-are-there-in-the-world
2 www.countryliving.com/shopping/news/a40276/mail-order-catalogs
3 www.johnbessant.org/casesac
4 www.johnbessant.org/casesmo
5 https://fortune.com/2022/03/08/mpesa-fintech-safaricom-innovation-kenya-africa-mobile-money-unbanked/

THE SCALE JOURNEY

Scaling isn't an automatic progression, the next step along a clearly marked and well-surfaced road. It's a journey.

To take a metaphor, it's an expedition into uncertain and (sometimes) hostile territory; not something you stumble through luckily finding a path: there isn't one. You have to hack through the jungle or find your way across the desert or ice field, inch your way up the mountainside, zigging and zagging and doubling back.

And the trouble is that getting to a successful pilot is only halfway along the journey. To stay with our geographical metaphor, we've successfully cut a path through the foothills, made our way through the uncharted lands to reach the base of the real mountain, which we have to climb. And now, as we stand in the sunlight looking up, we're aware of just how daunting a task it's going to be to climb this forbidding peak.

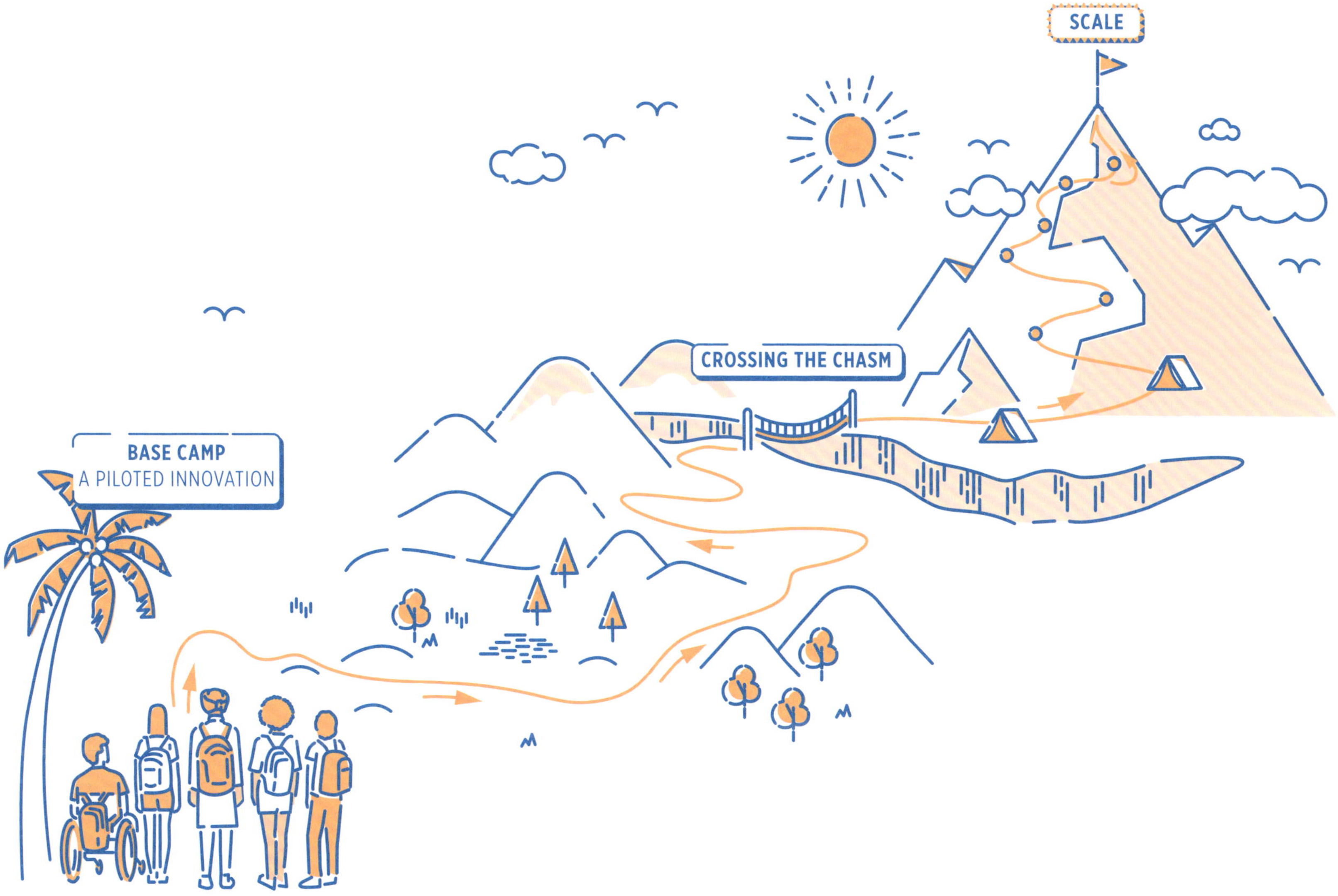
SCALE
CROSSING THE CHASM
BASE CAMP
A PILOTED INNOVATION

JOHN'S EVEREST STORY
PART 1

When I was a boy I loved my visits to my Uncle Bob's house. While my parents chatted in the dining room and my baby brother slept, I pored over a book full of black-and-white photos of Everest expeditions.

I was captivated by the way in which these intrepid explorers would inch their way up the treacherous slopes, the way they move crab-like up the slopes, setting up camps and leaving supplies for the next team of climbers to pick up and move farther upwards on their quest. The grainy black-and-white photos gave the book a chilling feeling; I could almost feel the wind lashing at my skin, hear the ice creaking and cracking in the background.

The descriptions of the narrow passes they had to traverse single file, the treacherous ice fields in which a missed step could drag an unsuspecting climber down into a deep crevasse. The painstaking climb using ice axes and pitons, ropes spinning like spider webs against sheer rock faces. And all the time the gasping for air, the need to carry heavy bottles of precious oxygen and the descriptions of what happens when people are deprived of air for too long.

Above all, I was struck by how many people were involved. Whilst the final triumphant pages showed Edmund Hillary and Sherpa mountaineer Tenzing Norgay on the summit, the book was full of the other members of the team, the ones who had to work together at various stages to enable the mountain to be conquered. And I was always saddened by the (long) list of names of the people who didn't make it back and whose corpses I imagined lying lonely and cold as the wind howled through the long dark Nepalese nights.

Expeditions like these have a lot in common – not least the need for meticulous planning and careful teamwork. There's plenty of stories of heroic failures – think Scott's fateful journey to the South Pole or Shackleton's somewhat madcap expedition into the Arctic. It's interesting; those stories have much to say about courage and ingenuity in the face of impossible odds, but the reality is that the successful expeditions – like Amundsen's South Pole journey – are often almost boring in their attention to detail and planning.

There's a lesson here for would-be innovators: a successful scaling expedition is going to need much more than just passion and drive.

WHAT'S THE PROBLEM?

STRATEGY, SYSTEMS AND SCALE

If we're serious about scaling our innovation, then we need to think strategically about it. It's not a simple afternoon excursion; it's this long uncertain journey, the scaling expedition. It's going to need a lot of planning.

First it needs a vision – and a vision of a system at the other end. It's not about an individual innovation made bigger, it's about creating a system. Think of some examples of success stories and it quickly becomes clear there was an underlying system vision.

Henry Ford's genius wasn't in inventing but in finding a scalable solution – the standardised car and manufacturing process which enabled a car for everyone. Thomas Edison deserves credit for much more than the light bulb – he thought beyond this, creating his General Electric Company to handle the system-level problem of what to plug the light bulb into, a network of power generation and distribution.

And in social innovation, Florence Nightingale's contribution was not just to improve patient care at a single hospital in Scutari.

IT'S NOT ABOUT AN INDIVIDUAL INNOVATION MADE BIGGER, IT'S ABOUT CREATING A SYSTEM.

FLORENCE NIGHTINGALE CASE STUDY

→ STRATEGIC SYSTEMS THINKERS

Complementary assets are those things which are needed to enable an innovation to scale – the 'what else and who else' of the story. Originally coined as a term by the economist David Teece.

She recognised the systemic nature of disease control and the importance of cleanliness and hygiene in all aspects of hospital operating procedures, plus she had the deep understanding of the role of evidence in helping convince others of the need for such systemic change.

They were all → STRATEGIC SYSTEMS THINKERS. And they also understood that while having a vision is essential, it isn't enough – you have to build that system to deliver value and that's going to take a lot of negotiating to get everyone in line. Thinking about complementary assets – who else and what else you need to enable your innovation to scale – is a key question for any innovator. Finding the right partners, forming relationships with them and welding the resulting network into a performing ecosystem isn't an easy task. That's what this book is about.

Whether you have the best idea since sliced bread (and Otto Rohwedder had a rocky 30-year climb to get his invention widely accepted) or you have the breakthrough concept which will really save the world, it's unlikely that the idea alone will have the power to scale. Instead you'll need a strategy for building a system – and a lot of uphill work to realise it.

STUCK IN THE MIDDLE WITH SCALE

The missing middle

When compared to the front end of innovation, scaling has relatively little guidance; that is why we wrote this book. But be prepared; compared to the rich library of guidance available around themes like ⊸ 'LEAN START-UP' DESIGN THINKING, human-centred design, and ideation, you are about to enter the relatively deserted shelves of materials which can help with the scaling journey. Keep this book close, you will find it a useful guide in the months and years ahead. But also, look out for those who have trodden this path before. Not all of their experiences will be applicable; their journey to the summit will have been on a different mountain, under different weather conditions and with different team members, often using different equipment. But they will have advice that is precious, so seek them out. All of them will be able to provide you with empathy and guidance regarding the other two middles of scaling.

WHAT'S THE PROBLEM?

**LEAN START-UP
DESIGN THINKING**

'Lean start-up' is a widely used methodology for guiding entrepreneurs through the key stages of developing their ideas into viable innovations.

Design thinking is a powerful methodology for developing innovations by including user perspectives from an early stage. For more on this see:

The messy middle

Mountains can become covered in fog that shrouds familiar objects in uncertainty, making you lose perspective, so you can't see where you are going.

Scaling is messy, and we mean, really messy. Getting to where you are now has been hard work and will have involved a number of pivots and changes, challenges and new insights. Those things won't change as you scale. What will change is the level of complexity you will be dealing with, in particular in building your Value Network. This is a messy process: be prepared for confusion and doubt. Be prepared for strained relationships and decisions made on the run without all the necessary facts. It will be messy, but you will deal with it!

The miserable middle

Professor Rosabeth Moss Kanter talks about the miserable middle in something that has been termed 'Kanter's law':

> *"Everything looks like a failure in the middle. Everyone loves inspiring beginnings and happy endings; it is just the middles that involve hard work."*

SCALING IS AN EXPEDITION, NOT AN AFTERNOON WALK IN THE PARK – SO YOU NEED TO BUILD RESILIENCE.

Back to the Everest expedition again: there may be moments of exhilaration, occasional highs as the team achieve something, feel they are making progress. But that has to be balanced with long days and nights in the bitter cold, wind lashing at the sides of the tent while you huddle inside desperately trying to heat water for a warming drink. Times when you crawl exhausted into your sleeping bag and wonder if you have the energy to make it through another day.

If you've been on a scaling journey you may recognise this. It's not a simple walk in the park: it's going to be a long hard slog. Your inspiring beginning is in the rear-view mirror and there's a difficult road ahead. It's important to prepare yourself as much as preparing the expedition. Build your personal resilience – and build a network of mentors and support, others who can help you make it through the miserable middle and up towards the happy ending when you have scaled that peak and achieved your scale vision.

WHAT'S THE PROBLEM?

HOW THE BOOK WORKS

The book is structured in the following way

PART 1

looks at the challenge of the scaling expedition in more detail and focuses on what we need to think about in preparing for our expedition. It provides an explanation to help us understand the scaling journey, drawing on the growing body of useful research in this field.

CHAPTER II looks at the scaling landscape and some initial mapping of the territory involved.

CHAPTER III explores the concept of value as something which is created and consumed as part of a multiplayer game.

CHAPTER IV explores this value theme further, looking at the idea of Value Networks and key roles within them.

CHAPTER V builds on the Value Network idea looking at the ways in which Value Networks can be built and

CHAPTER VI looks at some case examples – stories of success (and failure) mapped against this framework.

PART 2

moves from the theory and experience of others to focusing on execution – how will you handle your scaling challenge?

CHAPTER VII starts at what we call base camp and looks at the challenge of creating a Scale Panorama.

CHAPTER VIII takes a closer look at our solution and asks whether this innovation is really ready to scale.

CHAPTER IX looks at the question of how we organise for the scaling journey and whether we are ready to scale.

CHAPTER X returns to the idea of Value Networks and focuses on the first group of key roles – the 'Bookends' of Value Creators, Value Consumers and Value Captors.

CHAPTER XI explores the next group of roles – the 'Movers' – and how Value Channels, Value Conveyors and Value Coordinators operate.

CHAPTER XII Finally we look at the last group of roles – the 'Shapers' that delineate the boundaries of our Value Network. We explore the Value Competitors, Value Complementors and Value Cartographers in our network.

CHAPTER XIII Having mapped our roles in the network we look in this chapter at how they can be configured and organised to support scaling our innovation.

CHAPTER XIV In this chapter we bring all the elements together and create a scale strategy – planning our route to scale, identifying our priorities, etc.

Finally, there's a short afterword which explores emerging themes and questions around scaling innovation.

WHAT'S THE PROBLEM?

HOW TO USE THE BOOK

Don't get too comfortable! We've designed this as a playbook, a workbook, a resource which will help you think through and work on your own scaling expedition. Think of it as your diary/planner/notebook/expedition journal – something to accompany you on your journey to scale. If you're familiar with *The Hitchhiker's Guide to the Galaxy* then this is where we say 'Don't panic!' before offering a wide range of tools and techniques to help you in your expedition. (If you're not familiar with *The Hitchhiker's Guide to the Galaxy,* then think Tripadvisor or any of the other websites which help you prepare for going somewhere you've never been before, sharing tips, tricks and helpful advice.)

CHAPTER I — SUMMARY
WHAT YOU HAVE LEARNED IN THIS CHAPTER

▷ The challenge of scale – innovations which make it as far as being viable solutions do not always scale effectively.

▷ Scaling innovation is a long-term expedition into uncertain territory – and needs a strategy.

▷ Successful scaling depends on having a viable solution, which can be scaled, an organisation which can support the journey and the assembly of a network of complementary players to deliver value.

▷ It requires taking a systems perspective.

MAPPING THE JOURNEY TO SCALE

Scaling innovation is a major undertaking, a journey into uncertain territory. In this chapter we review what we've learned from research and particularly hard-won experience. The good news is that while we don't have full GPS precision, we do have some serviceable charts which at least give us a clear idea of the challenges which lie ahead.

FOR A LONG EXPEDITION INTO THE UNKNOWN YOU'RE GOING TO NEED SOME KIND OF MAP AND A RANGE OF TOOLS

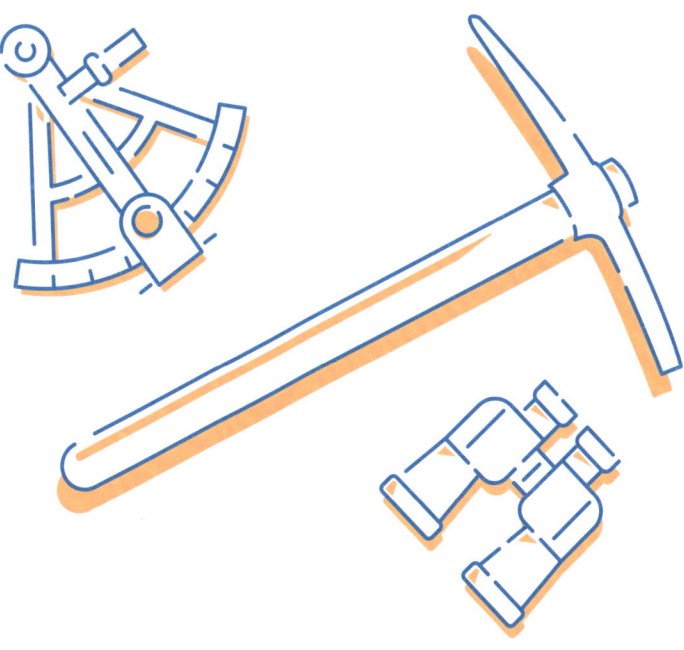

PLANNING THE EXPEDITION

It makes sense to think of the journey to scale not as a simple excursion but a major expedition, one which needs careful forethought and planning. As we sit around the table trying to imagine our ascent of Innovation Mountain we should go through our checklist of key points. We're going to need to consider a number of themes.

PART 1   PREPARING FOR THE SCALING EXPEDITION

Let's look at little more closely at each of these and what research and experience tells us about them.

IT TAKES TIME

"Overnight success stories take a long time."
STEVE JOBS

"There are no quick wins in business – it takes years to become an overnight success."
RICHARD BRANSON

MAPPING THE JOURNEY TO SCALE

"In the digital age of 'overnight' success stories such as Facebook, the hard slog is easily overlooked."
JAMES DYSON

"It took about 10 years for Shopify to be an overnight success."
TOBIAS LUTKE

"Ignore the early adopter critics that never have enough to play with. Ignore your investors that want proven tactics and predictable instant results. Listen instead to your real customers, to your vision and make something for the long haul. Because that's how long it's going to take, guys."
SETH GODIN

"Nothing is ever quick. You have to grow an audience, keep them engaged, give them a reason to keep coming back so it will never be an overnight success. Have patience!"
KAREN CIVIL

THE BIRTH OF THE BIKE

CASH PROGRAMMING IN THE FOOD ASSISTANCE SECTOR

TIP
Microfinance Barometer, 2018.

Once launched, new ideas often take a long time to have an impact. 🔗 *Think about the bicycle:* it was invented around 1817 by Baron Karl von Drais who certainly had a clear vision for what he was trying to achieve – affordable personal transportation for everyone. But it took another 60 years to make that dream a reality. Or look at the experience of Frederic Tudor, the 'Ice King' of Boston, who pioneered the global ice industry in the 19th century. His first (unsuccessful) voyage in 1806 took a shipload of ice to Martinique where its frosty reception had nothing to do with the product in his ship's hold. The problem was that there wasn't anywhere to store it when it arrived: the local people had no ice houses. It took another 10 years, all his family's money and a spell in debtor's prison before he finally succeeded in creating an industry which, in its heyday, was cutting and shipping close to a million tonnes of ice every year.

Timescales remain stubbornly long, even as technology life cycles shorten. For example, in the field of 🔗 *humanitarian aid,* the idea of giving people money instead of food can be traced back to experiments in the early 1980s. However, it took another 20 years before this moved to the mainstream – and even then it took the impact of the dreadful 2004 Indian Ocean tsunami to kick-start the diffusion to scale. Or in microfinance, a high-impact social innovation which took four decades to reach the scale it has today, now serving over 150 million people who would otherwise lack access to capital to start their small-scale ventures.

Oral rehydration therapy was developed in the 1940s but it wasn't until the Bangladesh refugee crisis in the 1970s that it became widely used. And Norman Borlaug, who developed high-yield, disease-resistant wheat varieties while working in Mexico in the 1940s and 50s, was nearly pushed out of the sector by his employer before his innovations started to show their full potential and contributed to the Green Revolution in Asia starting in the 1960s.

Timescales and timing matter in scaling innovation – something which helps explain the fate of Better Place (→ p. 14–15). The idea – battery swap technology – is a good one, but the world wasn't ready for it back in 2011. Too many pieces of the puzzle needed to come together and Shai Agassi simply ran out of time. (Interestingly enough, his idea lives on; there is renewed focus on battery swap systems especially in sectors where there is a need for high recharge rates and where drivers don't

MAPPING THE JOURNEY TO SCALE

have time to wait for their batteries to be recharged. Taxi services in and around big Chinese cities are a good example, and several firms now operate 🔗 *battery swap* systems at scale.)

So, if it's going to take a while to move to scale then we'll need to do more than just pat our innovation on the head and send it on its way. We need a strategy; a long-term plan for how it will happen.

🔗 BATTERY SWAPPING CASE STUDY

VALUE PROPOSITIONS

Any innovation begins life as a value proposition – a theory about what others will find useful in the new thing. Developing the innovation involves testing the truth (or otherwise) of this proposition and positing towards a solution which really does deliver value.

IT'S ABOUT HAVING A SCALABLE SOLUTION

One of the risks in starting out on the journey to scale is that we don't actually have a solution that can be scaled. We might have worked hard to develop our prototype and test it to the point that we can demonstrate there is demand and that it works. We're no longer in the realms of theory, thinking about VALUE PROPOSITIONS – we know our innovation can and does create value for someone. But can we scale this? And if so, which pathway will we take?

→ **FRANCHISING**

Franchising is a business model where a franchisor grants a franchisee the right to operate their established brand and business system in exchange for fees and ongoing support.

For the McDonald brothers, the challenge was to take their 'Speedee Service System', which was delighting customers in a small corner of California, and spread it. It took the vision of Ray Kroc to help them do so and the route which he chose was → FRANCHISING – defining the format and operations tightly and then repeatedly selling the concept to investors across the country and eventually around the world. That's one reason why McDonald's always looks so familiar; its pathway to scale has been replication, a bit like cells multiplying according to a tight genetic blueprint.

For Clive Sinclair, the pathway to scale for his home computer, the ZX80, was through hobby communities where word of mouth counted for a lot. This gave him initial acceleration so that he was able to jump the chasm from these very early adopters to a mainstream market. He is rightly recognised as a pioneer in establishing the market for personal computers, but when he tried to use the same model for his electromobility solution (the ⊸ SINCLAIR C5) it failed dismally.

For Netflix, the early model of using the postal service to grow their video rental business offered a limited route to scale. But spotting the technical possibilities emerg-

SINCLAIR C5 STORY

A good analysis of the C5 story can be found here:

Marks, A.P. (1989). The Sinclair C5 – An Investigation into its Development, Launch, and Subsequent Failure. European Journal of Marketing, 23(1), 61–71.

MAPPING THE JOURNEY TO SCALE

ing around streaming music pointed the way to a very different approach – online streaming – which enabled them to move beyond the geographic limits of the US continent and eventually to become a global player in video streaming.

There is no single pathway to scale, but a number of potential routes involving different players.

There are also different end points; innovations can be scaled via different routes with different degrees of control over how they are sustained in the long-term. This ranges from selling an innovation through to options like franchising and licensing where others sell it, to releasing the innovation in OPEN-SOURCE form and inviting others to modify and use it in whatever ways they wish.

In similar fashion the degree of change varies. Innovations don't remain the same over their lifetime; as many researchers point out what is being adopted and diffused will change as a result of that process. As an innovation scales it may remain largely in the same form as originally developed, it may be optimised to improve along the original design trajectory or it may

THERE IS NO SINGLE PATHWAY TO SCALE, BUT A NUMBER OF POTENTIAL JOURNEYS INVOLVING DIFFERENT PLAYERS.

OPEN SOURCE

Open source refers to innovations which are freely available and which can be modified and shared with others. It's particularly used to refer to software where users are encouraged to add to the stock of knowledge about a product to improve it. Linux is a good example of an open-source approach.

PART 1 PREPARING FOR THE SCALING EXPEDITION

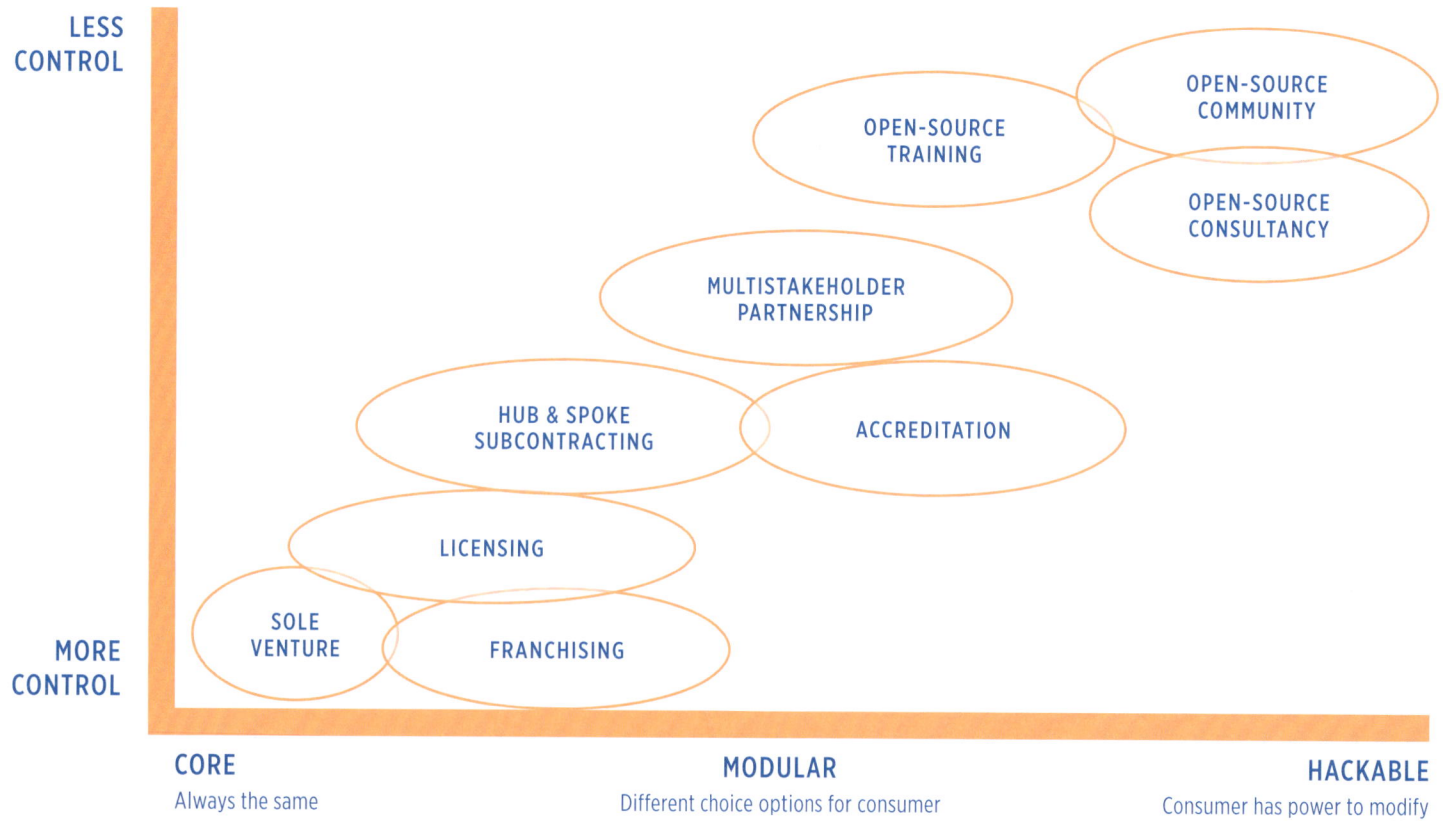

be significantly modified to add new functions. It will almost certainly undergo adaptations to match it to different contexts and after a sustained period of use may give rise to subsequent major new generations of the innovation.

IT'S ABOUT HAVING THE RIGHT ORGANISATION FOR SCALE

Think about a start-up team around a new venture and the picture probably forming in your mind's eye is a small tight-knit group who are passionate about what they do, to the point that they don't mind putting in the long nights and crashing out to sleep amidst the wreckage of half-eaten pizza and cold coffee, their wonderful ideas finally hammered out on the white board behind them. It's the stuff of TV dramas which highlight role models for how the process of developing a venture unfolds. We know that venture capitalists put a great deal of faith in the founding team, not just their ideas, and we know that it isn't a matter of lone geniuses but of interplay. Indeed the makeup of the team needs diversity; the cast of characters whose interaction makes the venture succeed: think Lennon and McCartney, Jobs and Wozniak, Bill Hewlett and Dave Packard, not forgetting that it was Brownie Wise who enabled Earl Tupper to scale his innovation.

The trouble is that whilst this team was the right one to get the venture off the ground, it may not necessarily be the right one for the scaling expedition. For a start there are going to be new skills and new knowledge that the team needs which will require recruiting new members. And they may not have the same values or founding passion – which can put a strain on the team dynamics. In some cases there may be clashes between founders and new members, or founders and the new board, which cause one or the other to leave – that's a familiar story as innovation teams try to move to scale.

Then there's the sheer organisational mechanics of handling growth – the number of people gets bigger and there's differentiation in the roles they need to play. Simply holding this together with the glue of shared passion may not be enough. Research on the growth of ventures often talks about a series of crises – turning points – through which the organisation has to go, and this early one of expanding numbers and the need for more formal organisation is a major problem area.

GROWTH CHALLENGES
Handling growth requires more than shared passion; organisational mechanics and role differentiation become crucial. This expansion phase often involves crises and turning points for the venture's development.

MODELS FOR SCALING
THE EXAMPLE OF ALCOHOLICS ANONYMOUS

There are many types of organisational models available to use for scaling. Alcoholics Anonymous is a good example of how value has been scaled significantly using a network and small headquarters approach.

- ▷ Addiction destroys the value in people's lives, and finding a way through it so that it is controlled is one of the most valuable achievements that any addict can make in their lives.

- ▷ Alcoholics Anonymous (AA) developed a process innovation based around 12 steps to help addicts control their addictions. From its start in Akron, Ohio, with two people, AA has become a mutual aid fellowship that is present in approximately 180 countries, with over 123,000 groups, and their literature has been translated into 100 languages.

- ▷ AA has managed to achieve this by being completely self-funded (they do not accept outside donations) and is primarily run by volunteers. Its New York-based 'General Service Office' which supports all of North America has less than 100 staff.

It's not always about growing bigger; scaling your innovation may not be the same as scaling your organisation. The value you are trying to create may not require you to expand your organisation significantly but it will require you to think hard about what has to change and why.

SCALING YOUR INNOVATION, MAY NOT REQUIRE SIGNIFICANT SCALING OF YOUR ORGANISATION.

MAPPING THE JOURNEY TO SCALE

The organisational model we choose needs to focus on our scaled operating model, how it is legally structured and governed, and how it facilitates scaling. We'll also need to design a strategy for ensuring this, as we don't want to become overly bureaucratic as we grow. We're aiming for what might be termed MINIMUM VIABLE BUREAUCRACY (MVB). And just as with our innovation, our organisation should be viewed as something to be iterated, subject to continuous improvement. Many successful scaled innovations have seen the organisational models built around them change multiple times.

How we set up legally will have a significant impact on how we scale, from the type of services we can provide, what types of revenue model we use, how profits and capital are distributed and taxed, and how intellectual property (IP) is registered and owned. It can also impact how we scale into other countries.

Beyond our legal registration, our scaling operating model for running the business at scale is also critical. It can be the difference between slow, linear growth and rapid, non-linear growth, as outlined in the Impact Hub case.

MINIMUM VIABLE BUREAUCRACY

Minimum viable bureaucracy (MVB) is having just enough process to make things work, but not too much to make it slow or rigid. It is making sure that you do not create overly bureaucratic policies, systems and processes as your organisation grows. Rather, you create these policies, systems and processes to be the bare minimum required to run your organisation effectively whilst retaining your agility and ability to adapt to changes quickly.

SCALE OPERATING MODEL
IMPACT HUB

The Impact Hub movement is a social enterprise co-working space and incubator. It was started in North London in 2005 by a group of friends. Its early days saw struggles, but wide levels of interest not only in the UK, but across Europe and around the world as well.

- ▷ Fairly early on the accreditation model was agreed on to be the best way forward. Those seeking to set up an Impact Hub would be provided guidance from the founding team and, if they achieved the right indicators, were accredited as Impact Hubs. This model is what we would call a hub-and-spoke model where the centre is responsible for supporting the establishment of each new Impact Hub across the planet.

- ▷ The outcome was a slow and linear growth trajectory, and a core team that was close to burnout. This led to the development of a different model, where the accreditation process was devolved to individual hubs. Those wanting to set up a new hub would now be accompanied on the process by two other hubs (chosen for geographical proximity and contextual similarity). This unlocked a non-linear growth path and enabled the maintenance of a small HQ. Impact Hub is now present in 50 countries, serving over 21 million customers and beneficiaries.

MAPPING THE JOURNEY TO SCALE

EPAI MODEL

(diagram showing arc with stages: Epai, EPai, EPAi, EPAI, ePAI, epAI, RIP)

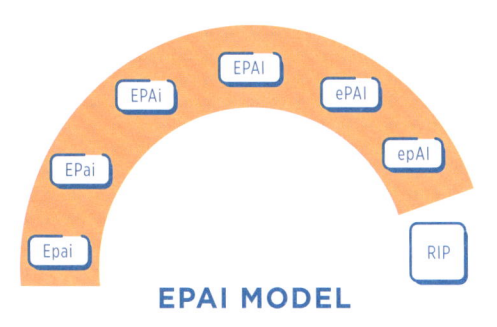

MINIMUM VIABLE PRODUCT (MVP)

is a key concept in the 'lean start-up methodology. It refers to the simplest form of prototype which can be used to test your value proposition on a market – in practice this could be a simple sketch or a mockup of a computer screen or a simple working model.

For more on MVP see:

(QR code)

Each organisational model will require different types of systems and processes to be built. A useful starting point is to think about stages – a helpful model for doing so is the *EPAI model* which looks at the entrepreneurship, product, administration and integration stages.

Each organisation starts out with an entrepreneur (or intrapreneur). We call this the 'Big E'. They then develop a product (this includes services and processes, etc.). At first this product is a prototype, a MINIMUM VIABLE PRODUCT (MVP) – let's call this 'Little p'. If it pilots well and can consistently deliver value, it becomes a 'Big P' product.

Once the product is selling or being adopted well, there is a need to build out some administration. Orders need to be fulfilled, finances need accounting, and processes need to be codified to establish standard operating procedures and organisational policies. More stuff which requires more human resources. Our start-up goes from having no administration to putting in some administration for workflow and key tasks ('Small a') to creating a significant amount of administration ('Big A').

PEAI TO EPAI

This model is an adaptation of Ichak Adizes PEAI model which looks at team roles. We have adapted it for the purposes of organisations lifecycles. Thanks to James Crowley who introduced Ian to PEAI originally.

> **CALCIFIED ZOMBIES**
>
> In competitive private sector markets, this may well lead to disruption and the death of the company. In oligopolistic, monopolistic, not-for-profit and public goods markets (e.g., state-run enterprises), this may not lead to disruption, but will lead to the erosion of value for Value Consumers. The organisation doesn't die, but becomes a calcified zombie, a place where the original entrepreneurial spirit and lifeblood of innovations have died, but the host body carries on delivering ever diminishing value.

This isn't the end of the organisational journey. As things scale we might start producing different versions of our product, start accessing new markets; in doing so we need to ensure that our systems still work effectively together. This is called integration and the challenge is to ensure that as we move from 'Little i' to 'Big I' we don't trap ourselves into a cookie-cutter approach where we assume that one size fits all.

The risk is that once an organisation reaches this stage the drive for efficiency and uniformity can destroy the entrepreneurial spirit at its heart: our 'Large E' becomes a 'Small e' as entrepreneurship is pushed to the margins, our organisation becomes increasingly rigid and we may see a dramatic tail off in innovation. And then our 'Big P' becomes a 'Small p' as we fail to refresh existing products and produce new ones, and the organisation starts to FALTER and ultimately fail.

This journey isn't inevitable; the key is to resist getting to the stage where systems and processes stifle innovation. This is why we place so much emphasis on the idea of MVB.

NETFLIX:
CULTURE DECK CASE STUDY ACHIEVING MVB

Netflix identified similar issues that we identify in the EPAI model and explained them in their 'culture deck', which all prospective employees are shown. To combat bureaucratisation, they sought to have the right high-performing people in place. In the deck they outline that they are successful by recruiting and retaining 'the right people'. And instead of a 'culture of process adherence', they created of 'culture of freedom and responsibility, innovation and self discipline'.

They provide significant freedom to make decisions based on principles and context. Allowing staff to make informed and responsible judgements. Later in the deck they proclaim that their 'model is to increase employee freedom as we grow, rather than limit it'.

This meant that they could keep their policies short and dynamic. Such as this one.

By providing staff with context-based examples to inform decision making, they are able to achieve MVB for their expensing, entertainment, gifts and travel policy.

NETFLIX POLICIES FOR EXPENSING, ENTERTAINMENT, GIFTS AND TRAVEL

Act in Netflix's Best Interests.

Organisational capabilities

As Jim Collins observed in his best-selling book, **GOOD TO GREAT**, focusing on what is core is key for long-term success. Which core capabilities will help us successfully scale? And how can we ensure that we are building them? In particular we're looking for those capabilities which are VRIN:

- Valuable: They produce more value for us than competitors
- Rare: They are not readily available to others
- Inimitable: They can't be copied easily
- Non-substitutable: Other capabilities or resources can't be used instead

By assessing whether they are **VRIN** gives us a way of ensuring we can scale in ways competitors can't.

Culture

Culture is one of those tricky words which can mean many different things to different people. But in its simplest form it's a way of describing 'the way we do things round here' in our organisation – the pattern of beliefs which create the norms which guide our behaviour.

THE POWER OF ORGANISATIONAL CULTURE

Collins, J. (2001). Good to great: Why some companies make the leap…and others don't. New York: Harper Collins.

THE RESOURCE-BASED VIEW OF THE FIRM

Barney, J. (1991). Firm resources and sustained competitive advantage. Journal of Management, 17(1): 99–120.

VRIN DENOTES VALUABLE, RARE, INIMITABLE, AND NON-SUBSTITUTABLE ATTRIBUTES THAT CONFER A COMPETITIVE ADVANTAGE.

MAPPING THE JOURNEY TO SCALE

CULTURAL WEB*

6 CONTROL SYSTEMS
How autonomous are staff in decision making?

2 POWER STRUCTURES
How is formal and informal power structured in the organisation?

5 RITUALS AND ROUTINES
What rituals and routines have been developed? Are they still working for their intended purposes?

1 STORIES
What are the prevalent stories that are told in your organisation, and what does it say about you?

7 PARADIGM
How would you describe the dominant world view in the organisation, is it diverse or monochromatic?

3 SYMBOLS
What are the status symbols, or other symbols of what is important and what conveys inclusion and power?

4 ORGANISATIONAL STRUCTURE
Have you already started to create hierarchies? Are there silos developing?

* Johnson, G., Scholes, K. & Whittington, R. (2008). Exploring corporate strategy, 8th edition, Harlow et al.: Pearson Education Limited.

PIRATES
Rule-breakers, convention-ignorers, those who push the boundaries and innovate and don't like structure

PRIVATEERS
Pirates who can play by the petty officer rules when it makes strategic sense

PETTY OFFICERS
Rule-adherers, process- and policy-followers

PIRATES IN THE NAVY

Viki, T. (2020). Pirates In The Navy: How Innovators Lead Transformation. London: Unbound Publishing.

Tendayi Viki guides the reader through the idea of intrapreneurs being pirates, but trying to work in large organisations that feel like being in the Navy. It riffs off the legendary story of Steve Jobs putting a pirate flag outside his development office when he returned to Apple, stating, "it is more fun to be a pirate than to join the Navy."

Team roles

Everyone knows about pirates. They break rules, go against convention and are not happy with the status quo. And they give us a nice metaphor for one kind of organisational role which is useful in scaling innovation: we need **RULE-BREAKERS** who challenge in order to get something new to happen.

Privateers are an interesting hybrid. Originally a privateer was a kind of licenced pirate – pirates who commanded their own ships but, in times of war, could be commissioned by the navy to help them achieve their objectives. (Sir Francis Drake is perhaps the most famous example of a privateer.)

But we also need to balance this with other roles – for example that of the petty officer. A petty officer is a rank in the navy and their role is to ensure rules get followed; they have set processes and systems and stick to them. They reinforce and work within the established structure.

MAPPING THE JOURNEY TO SCALE

> **SMART ORGANISATIONS CONNECT WITH MENTORS TO HELP THEM ON THEIR JOURNEY – NOT JUST FOR MORAL SUPPORT AND ENCOURAGEMENT, BUT ALSO BY ACTING AS CHALLENGING AND CRITICAL FRIENDS.**

When our organisation was in start-up mode creating our innovation, we needed pirates breaking rules and trying the outrageous (obviously ethically!). But when it comes to scaling, we have to plug into the Value Network around us, and we have to start developing policies and processes.

This means that we need to start bringing on board new people and setting up incentive structures that start rewarding different behaviours. We don't want to go to the extreme (as outlined in the EPAI model) where there are only petty officers at the helm. But we do need to start recruiting and incentivising our team to start behaving like privateers.

Mentoring

You may not always be able to get the right people in-house. Our experience and research show that a critical part of building your capability is access to external advice from 'guides'. Mentoring is worth its weight in gold to many scaling organisations since it offers the chance to trade on someone else's hard-won experience. In our metaphorical ascent of Innovation Mountain it will be very helpful to have some guides who know the ins and outs of making such a journey – they understand the local weather conditions, the different paths and routes available and a host of other valuable lore.

Smart organisations connect with mentors to help them on their journey – not just for moral support and encouragement, but also by acting as challenging and critical friends.

Financial model

Our financial model is critical for scaling, not least because accountants (ours and those of potential investors) will look carefully at our revenue and costs, our balance sheet and our cash flow. Scaling puts intense pressure on cash flow, so developing performing and scalable revenue models whilst managing costs to ensure that we are able to smooth out our cash flow will be critical to remaining viable as we scale.

For most innovations, revenue will often be less than costs as we scale, so we'll need injections of funds, either through investment, loans or grants. For the lucky few (and we really do mean lucky), investment can be so significant that they just fill the chasm with cash and can then walk straight over it. This is why – particularly for tech companies relying on network effects – we hear stories of companies going to scale and reaching IPO without ever making revenues exceed costs. However, the vast majority of organisations and businesses don't have this luxury, so establishing performing revenue models and well-managed cost models are critical as we scale.

There isn't a one-size-fits-all revenue model; instead we need to aim for a good fit with our operating circumstances. For example, the type of market we operate in will often determine what type of revenue model we can use. → VALUE CONSUMERS that are governments or businesses will often use contracts with significant gaps between payments, whilst 'base of the pyramid' consumers with limited disposable income will often only be able to afford micropayments on a daily or weekly basis. This impacts the revenue model we can use and will have significant effects on our cash flow and need for upfront investments.

Markets also have dominant revenue models which Value Consumers will expect. For instance, when news-

---

→ **VALUE CONSUMERS**

are those people who take value from our innovation. We discuss this and other roles in Chapter IV.

MAPPING THE JOURNEY TO SCALE

papers were the primary way of reading the news, there was an expectation that Value Consumers would pay for the newspaper. The switch to online news consumption stripped out large parts of the cost for writing and disseminating news. This allowed news to be delivered solely based on advertising as a revenue stream, creating the expectation that news should be free. The norm has therefore switched from Value Consumers paying for newspapers to accessing their news for free online, even from news outlets that still print and sell physical newspapers.

Public and social goods can be hard to create a revenue model for. An example is the struggle faced by many open-source ○ DIGITAL PUBLIC GOODS AND INFRASTRUCTURE INNOVATIONS. And, of course, the level of competition in a market will heavily influence the price point you can sell at and what revenue model is the most competitive.

→ COST MODELS bring their own challenges; the need to add so much in the way of resources and staff to build capabilities means that costs can quickly go out of control. In 2022, FTX, a former star of the cryptocurrency world that had scaled dramatically, suddenly collapsed.

DIGITAL PUBLIC GOODS AND INFRASTRUCTURE INNOVATIONS

For example, Frontline SMS, was a software tool for using sms to broadcast and receive messages to a mass audience for issues such as public health. It was free to download and use, and was used by many charities across the globe. However, it could not sustain itself easily, and eventually closed down in 2021.

They have an interesting blog of their experience here:

→ COST MODEL

A cost model is a way of representing all the elements in a business which cost it money – for example buying raw materials, paying staff, paying for the use of marketing channels, etc. It is sometimes called the 'cost structure' of an enterprise and is important because without a clear understanding of costs and their drivers, it is impossible to control the cash flow.

The stories of FTX profligacy, such as a $40 million apartment and private jet for the co-founder, came to the fore as the company spiralled towards bankruptcy. Rapid growth, particularly when it is fuelled more by investment than earned revenue, can lead to extravagances that are detrimental to scaling.

Cost minimisation doesn't have to mean cutting back; it can also emerge as a result of clever partnerships, particularly in regard to insourcing, outsourcing and how we can leverage other entities in our network.

IT'S ABOUT 'CROSSING THE CHASM'

As we saw in the last chapter, we are in the business of planning a long-term expedition, not an afternoon excursion. So it helps to think ahead, get some reconnaissance on the likely terrain and where the obstacles and roadblocks might lie. In terms of map-making, even a rough sketch is better than no chart at all.

Fortunately we have a good set of charts to help us plan our ascent built on our understanding of the process of adoption and diffusion of innovation. People don't simply accept changes; instead there's a pattern in which some are enthusiastic early adopters whilst others may take a long while to make up their minds. Whether we are talking about toothpaste, concierge services or high-technology machinery, the same pattern will appear and it takes the form of an S-curve.

A TYPICAL S-CURVE FOR DIFFUSION OF AN INNOVATION

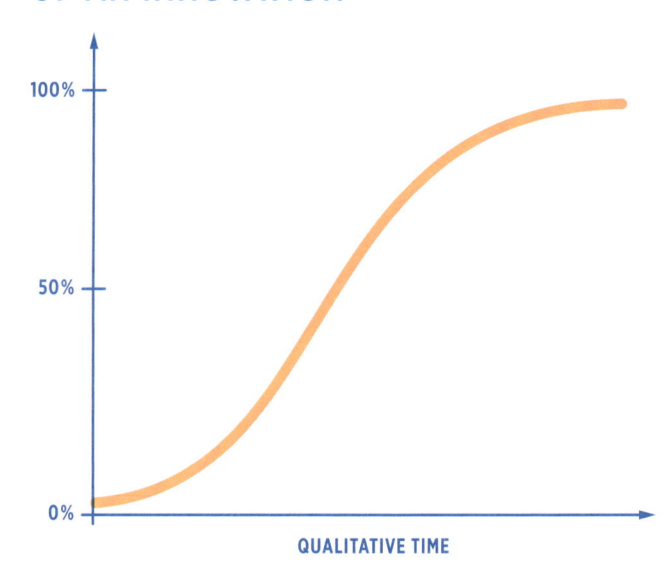

S-CURVE
Innovation's adoption curve: slow start, rapid growth, saturation.

Understanding what shapes this S-curve and the underlying adoption patterns was the life's work of Everett Rogers. It offers us some powerful clues about adoption. He saw it in terms of a communication process and a key point here is that different people perceive the characteristics of an innovation (the message) in different ways. Whether or not our innovation is the best new thing since the invention of sliced bread is not the issue – it is how others perceive it which matters. In particular, five sets of factors are important.

COMPLEXITY CAN HAMPER DIFFUSION, AS THE FAILURE OF THE GOOGLE TV REMOTE CONTROL WITH 88 BUTTONS SHOWS.

CHECKLIST
Rogers lists five innovation characteristics and these provide a helpful checklist

- 1. Relative advantage – can we prove a difference in performance on some dimension?

- 2. Observability – can we show the benefits – seeing is believing?

- 3. Complexity – can we present our idea in simple form?

- 4. Trialability – can we offer the chance of a 'test drive' before requiring a full commitment?

- 5. Compatibility – how well does the new thing fit into the (potential) user's world?

This checklist also helps us understand why things often go wrong in diffusion. Consider the question of complexity – Google TV was one of their less successful ventures and it failed in part because it was perceived as too complex. Something exemplified in the remote controller which Sony produced to fit the system which had no less than 88 buttons for different functions!

Rogers's work didn't just focus on perceptions of the innovation – it also extended to the innovator. People trust things which they perceive as coming from someone like them (homophily) and they are suspicious of things which come from outside their world. That's one reason why Brownie Wise was so important in the successful scaling of Tupperware – she was perceived by her market (mainly homemakers attending Tupperware parties) as someone just like them: a busy single parent trying to balance a busy life.

And people are not all the same – they differ widely in their willingness to take on new ideas. Rogers suggested that they are distributed over time and he even gave names to the different categories. These are:

- *'Innovators' – people who are likely to take on any new idea simply because of its novelty*

- *'Early adopters' – those who evaluate the innovation carefully but then are early to adopt*

- *'Early majority' – these follow early adopters and build the momentum behind the innovation*

- *'Late majority' – these are followers who go with the rest of the population once momentum has been established*

- *'Laggards' – people who resist change and may never adopt or do so very late in the day*

TYPES OF INNOVATION ADOPTER

TYPES OF INNOVATION ADOPTER

Innovation adopters help to understand how individuals or groups react to new ideas or innovations.

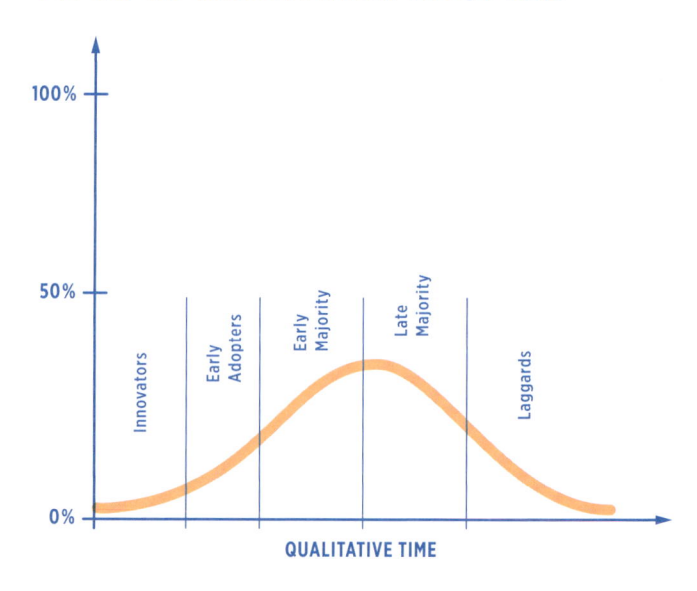

MAPPING THE JOURNEY TO SCALE

Which brings us to the big scaling question of how we 'cross the chasm'. As Rogers noted, there are always some people (he called them innovators) who will adopt something new simply because it's new. Think about the folk who camped all night outside Apple stores to make sure they got their hands on the latest MacBook, iPad or iPhone.

But beyond those are the key segment: the early adopters. These people think carefully before adopting something new – but when they do, others will follow. They are the Joneses with whom we try to keep up. The challenge in scaling innovation is how to cross this chasm – to move from those early adopters into the mainstream. This chasm can also become a valley of death in these instances as fledgling start-ups run out of cash, so it is doubly important to find a way across it.

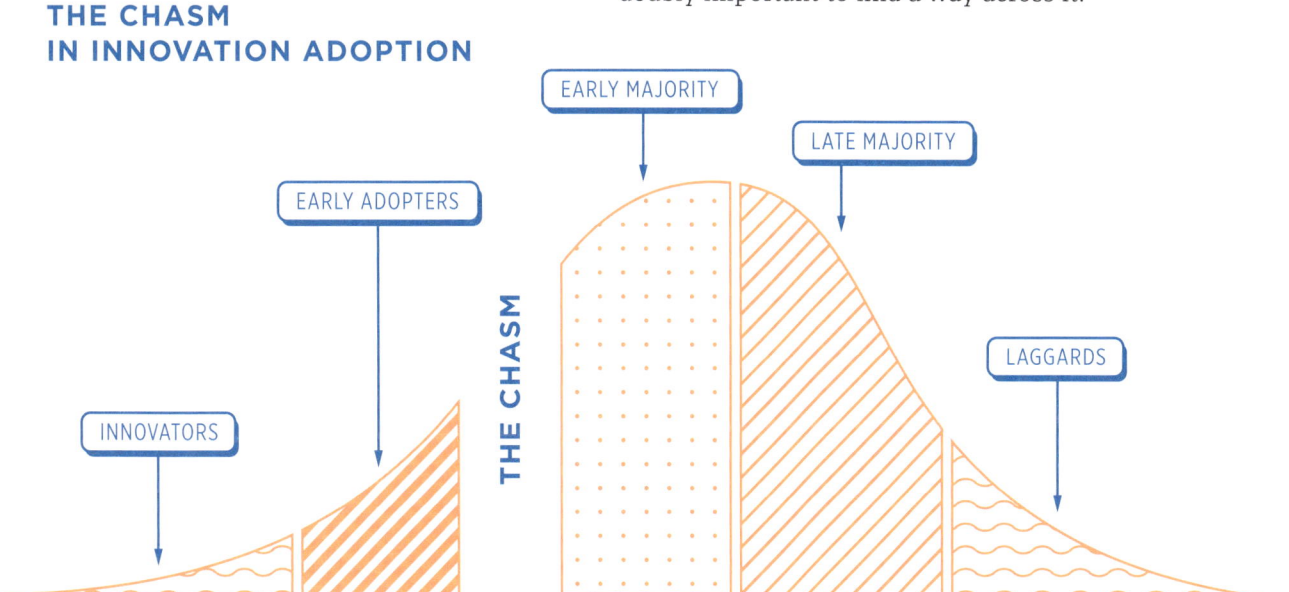

THE CHASM IN INNOVATION ADOPTION

INNOVATORS
EARLY ADOPTERS
EARLY MAJORITY
LATE MAJORITY
LAGGARDS

THE CHASM

THE CHASM

The challenge in scaling innovation is to bridge this gap – to move from early adopters to the mainstream.

THE POWER OF EVIDENCE

For more on this see 'Impact Evidence and Beyond: Using Evidence to Drive Adoption of Humanitarian Innovations', ELRHA, 2021

RESEARCH

Rogers, E. M. (1962). Diffusion of Innovations. New York: Free Press.

In a physical, geographical sense we might imagine a deep and treacherous ravine or crevasse over which we have to go – there is no route around it. We're going to need to find some way of bridging this, and recognise that our early attempts may be very risky; think flimsy rope bridges prone to shaking and slippage. So how do we cross the chasm?

Research has shown that several things can help us in constructing our bridge across the chasm, even if it still resembles a series of planks swinging precariously held up by flimsy ropes! For example, the role of EVIDENCE – the 'seeing-is-believing'-effect. The more we can show that our innovation really does make a difference, the more we can move people towards a favourable position in adopting it. We can help this process through endorsement – think about toothpaste and count the number of times advertisements invoke white-coated dentists and oral surgeons to help promote adoption of a new brand. This is deliberate – we are influenced by opinion leaders and people we perceive as having expert knowledge. This also explains the explosion in companies using social media influencers to push their products.

Different sectors may require different levels of evidence as part of their scaling efforts. In highly regulated markets such as pharmaceuticals, we'll need strict animal and human subject scientific trials if we're to secure approval by regulators.

At the other end of the scale, evidence can be hearsay – using quotes from Value Consumers as part of the evidence. Such endorsements can play an important role. RESEARCH tells us that adoption is a social process: we are strongly influenced by people we perceive as trustworthy and by the experience of 'people like us'.

In aggregated form, this can be critical for the adoption decision-making process; that's why so many organisations make use of customer reviews on Google, Amazon, Tripadvisor and other platforms.

MAPPING THE JOURNEY TO SCALE

Working with users can also help with crossing the chasm. By definition, if users are involved in creating the innovation it's likely to fit their world (compatibility) and they have a stake in its success. And if the innovation originates from users' own experiences and frustrations then it's likely to match those of people like them and diffuse rapidly.

Betty Nesmith Graham was a typist who made mistakes. Her idea for Liquid Paper correction fluid spread fast amongst the thousands of other typists similarly annoyed by the problem of having to retype corrections. And Mandy Haberman's experience as a mother fighting a mountain of washing led her to invent (and millions of caregivers to adopt) a non-splash drinking cup for toddlers.

THE POWER OF CUSTOMER REVIEWS
AEROPRESS

▷ One of the key ways to 'prove' the value of your innovation as you scale is through customer reviews. These can either be on comparison websites, such as Tripadvisor or Trustpilot, or through your organisation using direct consumer quotes.

▷ A great example of this is AeroPress, a filtered-coffee innovation. They use quotes from both coffee experts and the ordinary public from very ordinary places to extol the virtues of their coffee press. It is not often that you see a quote from someone in the much-maligned town of Milton Keynes in the UK on the packaging of a global product, but by having a quote from an ordinary person in Milton Keynes, it gave credibility that 'normal people' were delighted with both the ease of use of the filter press and the quality of the coffee produced.

USERS MATTER IN INNOVATION

For an extended discussion of the role of users see von Hippel, E. (2018). Free Innovation, Cambridge MA: MIT Press.

IT'S ABOUT NETWORKS AND SYSTEMS THINKING

Innovation involves a number of elements: the key components of our extended business model, thinking about the value-creating network of key suppliers and resources, the understanding of the market and what it actually values and, not least, the financing to ensure the cash flow to make it work and stay alive.

Imagine yourself as the innovator who saw the potential in remote retailing, providing a service for those people who couldn't or wouldn't visit shops. It's a good idea, but to make it work you'd need to assemble a lot of pieces of the jigsaw puzzle. Selling is one thing, but you'd also need to think about plenty of other things: capturing and processing orders, arranging for stock to be available, storage and distribution, handling logistics over a large area and, very importantly, managing the cash flow so that you don't sit on lots of stock but manage to get paid up front.

You might think that was all part of Jeff Bezos's genius in setting up his Amazon empire, but in fact it's a model which predates him by almost a century. People like Messrs Sears and Roebuck pioneered the idea of remote retailing via the mail order catalogue, but theirs wasn't a single-component innovation: they built an ecosystem. And they were smart enough to recognise that they didn't need to own or control everything as long as they could orchestrate and coordinate it. Major manufacturers and other players then came into the ecosystem tent – all sharing in the value creation.

A key part of that innovation-implementation journey is going to be about identifying the Value Network we need – the additional players who will make up our system – and developing the working relationships with them so that the whole system can create value. In systems theory there's a concept called emergent properties, which basically says that in a well-functioning system the whole is greater than the sum of its parts.

Well-functioning systems don't deliver these emergent properties by accident – they require an input of energy to weave and hold the system together. So, we need to be clear that it's going to take a lot of energy on our part to make sure we have a system with the right elements being held together through the right relationships.

EMERGENT PROPERTIES

Innovation adopters help to understand how individuals or groups react to new ideas or innovations.

The lesson for scaling is to ensure that you have thought of the ecosystem that you will need and have in place mechanisms to help build it – partnerships, licences, strategic collaborations, etc. Without it even the best ideas may fail, as we saw in the case of Better Place.

We'll revisit this Value Network idea in the next chapter.

«

CHAPTER II — SUMMARY
WHAT YOU HAVE LEARNED IN THIS CHAPTER

▷ Scale matters: innovation is not just about start up and launch but the whole journey towards impact at scale.

▷ Making this journey takes time, so you need a strategy.

▷ The scaling journey is an expedition, not an excursion.

▷ Moving to scale requires having a solution which can be scaled.

▷ Making the journey needs a viable organisation to support scaling.

▷ Undertaking the journey requires an understanding of the scaling terrain and in particular strategies for crossing the chasm.

▷ Scaling innovation involves a system, so you need to learn how to assemble a Value Network.

CHAP III MANAGING THE SCALE EXPEDITION: THE POWER OF VALUE NETWORKS

Moving innovation to scale requires many complementary players working together as a system. Value creation involves more than a simple linear process; it is enacted by their interplay. So we need to understand how to configure ecosystems and in particular address the challenges of finding partners, forming relationships with them and getting the whole system to perform effectively.

TENZING NORGAY AND
EDMUND HILLARY

JOHN'S EVEREST STORY
PART 2

Back to John's early memories of the Everest expedition book.

One of the pleasures of reading and re-reading the Everest expedition book was the sense of climax building. Never mind that I knew the story; never mind that I'd read it many times before: I always loved arriving at the page near the end with a photograph of Hillary and Tenzing standing on the summit smiling out from the roof of the world. It was a grainy black-and-white photo set in sharp contrast to the white expanse of the other Himalayan peaks stretching to fill the space behind them. It was May 29, 1953 and 29,035 feet below them was the rest of a world looking on in amazement.

But even then I knew that theirs wasn't a solo act, the heroics of a couple of brave men doing something impossible. It was the product of teamwork and an achievement which owed everything to the many players on the team who'd done their part to make the expedition succeed.

Scaling innovation is like that Everest expedition. There's an alignment, a sense of common purpose and there's a carefully choreographed interplay of actions. Everyone contributes to the system and the result has emergent properties – the whole becomes greater than the sum of the parts. If innovation is about creating value from ideas, then scaling innovation is about enacting that value through a Value Network.

Just like any major expedition, the visible leaders who set foot on summits or plant flags on previously unconquered territory are a small part of a much bigger group. Success depends on having a whole ecosystem – a set of linked players all aligned to try and create and deliver value. And it doesn't take us long to realise that assembling and operating such an ecosystem is no small endeavour.

LEADING THE JOURNEY TO SCALE

Whilst Hillary and Tenzing were the first to set foot on the summit, the expedition as a whole was a much bigger operation and was formally led by Sir John Hunt. His role was to provide the focus and coordination of

> **IF INNOVATION IS ABOUT CREATING VALUE FROM IDEAS, THEN SCALING INNOVATION IS ABOUT ENACTING THAT VALUE THROUGH A VALUE NETWORK.**

the many different people and resources which came together to make the successful ascent.

It's the same with scaling innovation. As we saw in the previous chapter, we need a Value Network of multiple players. But simply throwing the elements together isn't enough – we need to orchestrate that system, bring it to life. And that process will depend on active direction and leadership.

BUILDING VALUE NETWORKS

Building such an effective system isn't an instant process. If we could take a reverse timeline and track back from the 'summit moment' to how an expedition was planned and executed we'd find a pattern of careful assembly. The ecosystem which enabled the successful ascent of the mountain involves a combination of formal contracts and informal collaborations, and is built using a variety of different approaches to create performing partnerships.

It's the same with bringing together the Value Network for the ascent of the Innovation Mountain – it's an active process of configuring and coordinating. We can think in terms of three core aspects of this system building:

○ *Finding: seeking out or being introduced to the players you need to succeed, scoping and building the network*

○ *Forming: making them into a co-operative system with a shared goal in which roles are clear, rewards and risks are shared, etc.*

○ *Performing: orchestrating its management and governance to ensure it delivers emergent properties – the whole is greater than the sum of the parts. This will involve a considerable degree of pivoting – adapting to changing circumstances. It's not something which can be designed and operated according to a fixed plan or contract*

GUIDANCE TO THE MOUNTAIN

It is not enough to simply put the elements together – we need to orchestrate the system, bring it to life. And this process depends on active leadership and guidance.

VALUE NETWORKS AND INNOVATION ECOSYSTEMS

The term → 'ECOSYSTEM' is increasingly used these days, so it's worth going back to its roots and being clear what we are talking about. It's a concept which comes originally from biological science and refers to "the complex of a community of organisms and its environment functioning as an ecological unit."*

It has been applied in many branches of natural science with the same focus on an interdependent collection of elements with a shared goal or purpose, for example in geography:

> An ecosystem is a geographic area where plants, animals, and other organisms, as well as weather and landscape, work together to form a bubble of life…Every factor in an ecosystem depends on every other factor, either directly or indirectly. (National Geographic Encyclopedia)

And in the organisational world, the word has increasingly come to be used to describe something in which multiple interdependent elements are linked to focus on a common purpose.

It's pretty clear that ecosystems don't just happen in the innovation world. In the physical world they take millions of years to settle into a viable pattern. And in the world of organisations it's going to involve much more than just assembling a set of components. It will need active management to secure the emergent properties.

ENACTING VALUE

Innovation is all about creating value from ideas. But value is a tricky concept. Even at the start of our innovation journey, when all we have is a value proposition, we need to think about our target user. We have a proposition – a theory of what might make a difference to them – but we need to test this out and draw in as much information about their perspective as possible. So we work our idea up into a prototype; we elaborate and test repeatedly, pivoting along the way. Finally we pilot and then launch.

→ **ECOSYSTEM**
"something (such as a network of businesses) considered to resemble an ecological ecosystem especially because of its complex interdependent parts"

* Definition of 'ecosystem' from the Merriam-Webster.com Dictionary (2023).

MANAGING THE SCALE EXPEDITION: THE POWER OF VALUE NETWORKS

> **ENACTING VALUE INVOLVES CONTINUING INTERACTION WITH A GROWING CAST OF STAKEHOLDERS; IT'S A MULTIPLAYER GAME.**

By then we have a solution: something which seems to work; something which seems to be valued by our pilot group of users. But as we've seen, that's only the halfway point. Now we have to scale – and more than ever that process will involve an agile interaction with the real world of markets and stakeholders, learning and changing as we go.

In other words, value isn't magically created by an innovation goose laying a golden egg, or an entrepreneurial alchemist stirring their potion to magically create gold. Value is enacted – worked out as we go along.

Enacting value involves continuing interaction with a growing cast of stakeholders; it's a multiplayer game. At its heart is our solution – the thing which incorporates our learning from interaction with our key users. This is the device through which we incorporate value and bring it to life. It starts out as a sketch – a germ of an idea; a value proposition that gradually comes to life.

In our expedition metaphor, this corresponds to the initial enthusiastic challenge phase: a small team finds an unconquered peak and dreams about the day they might stand on its summit. But that soon gives way to a

ENACTING VALUE
It begins as a sketch – a seed of an idea; a value proposition that gradually evolves into reality.

long round of discussions, bringing in more people and assembling a lot of information – about earlier attempts, weather and geological conditions, logistics challenges and, not least, who and how is it all going to be paid for. In the process, the simple 'lets pick up our ice axes and set off' changes into a much more detailed and thought-through plan, one which can be shared and discussed with an increasingly wide cast of characters who will be involved in the expedition. It's a process of pivoting and learning, distributed across an increasingly wide network of players, not all of whom will share the same enthusiasm or be motivated in the same way.

Sponsors may have a very different viewpoint from climbers; lawyers setting up insurance may take very different stances to those of the logistics team. For many of these relationships, it's not going to be a matter of giving orders or exerting control; instead it will involve negotiations and alignment, building performing partnerships out of sometimes adversarial starting conditions.

And the lines between players may blur; they can play multiple roles. A sponsor might also be a climbing enthusiast wanting to be part of the team. Someone on the logistics team might also be a keen photographer, interested to document (and publish) the story of the expedition.

What we're actually doing as we assemble the team is configuring a Value Network – an ecosystem of players who work together to enable us to create the value we're aiming for. We may not control them all; we may have to nudge and plead, negotiate and compromise. We're trying to manage our ecosystem – and that's the key to this book.

DIVERSE COLLABORATIONS

Sponsors and climbers may have divergent perspectives; lawyers and logistics teams may hold contrasting positions. These relationships require negotiation, alignment, and the building of productive partnerships, even in adversarial situations.

CHAPTER III — SUMMARY
WHAT YOU HAVE LEARNED IN THIS CHAPTER

▷ Moving innovation to scale requires many complementary players working together as a system.

▷ Value creation involves more than a simple linear process; it is enacted by their interplay.

▷ So we need to understand how to configure ecosystems and in particular address the challenges of finding partners, forming relationships with them and getting the whole system to perform effectively.

CHAP IV
CONFIGURING VALUE NETWORKS

This chapter explores nine key roles which are played in Value Networks and looks at the ways different players can change their roles or play multiple roles. Value is not something which is simply created in a linear fashion by a creator meeting the needs of a consumer. Rather it is enacted by the interplay between these various roles in a Value Network.

FINDING, FORMING AND PERFORMING

Moving innovation to scale requires us to assemble and configure a Value Network of complementary players. But this doesn't happen automatically; it needs us to pay attention to three key stages – finding, forming and performing.

The 'finding' stage is essentially about providing the momentum for bringing the network together and clearly defining its purpose. We need to be clear about what elements we have to assemble and what makes up a viable ecosystem. While doing this might be the result of trial and error, it's also something that others can help with – network brokers, gatekeepers, policy agents and facilitators.

The 'forming' stage involves building a kind of extended organisation with some structure to enable its operation. We call this part of your ecosystem your 'inner Value Network'.

FORMING THE VALUE NETWORK

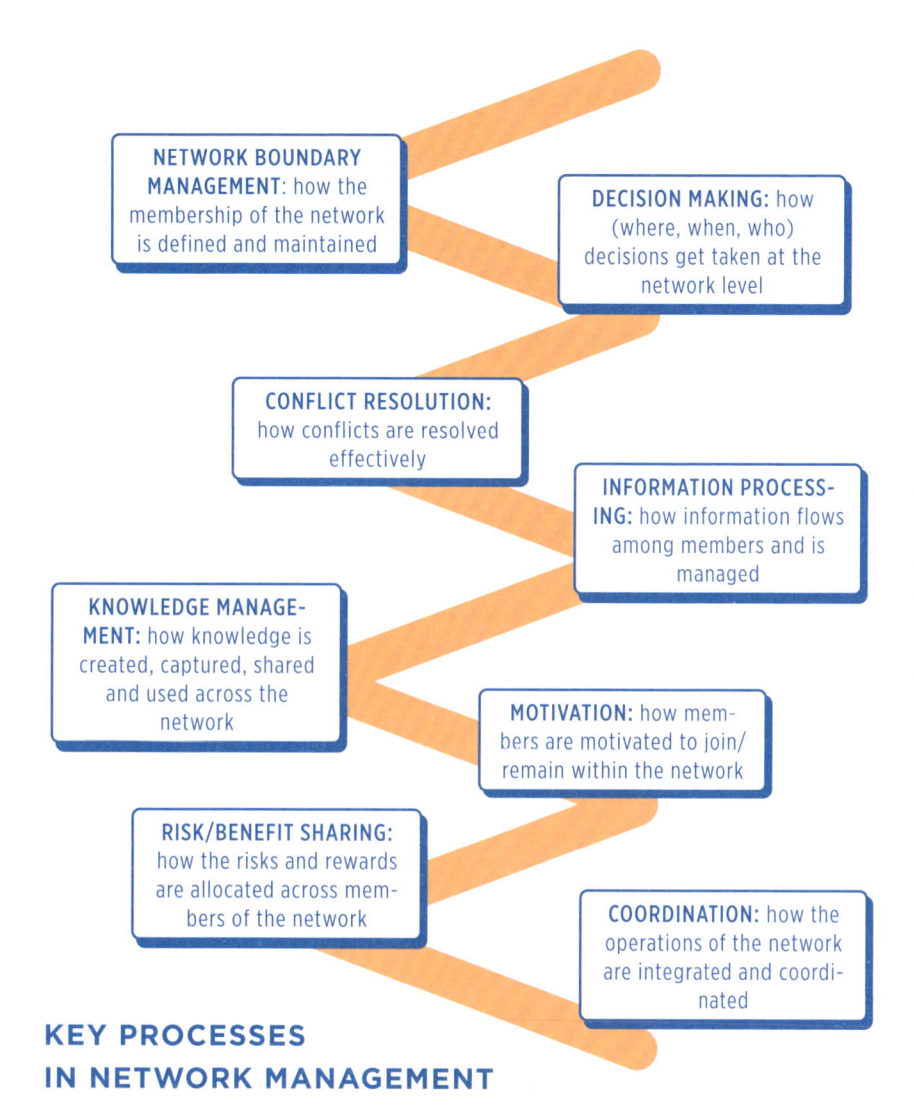

PART 1   PREPARING FOR THE SCALING EXPEDITION

NETWORK BOUNDARY MANAGEMENT: how the membership of the network is defined and maintained

DECISION MAKING: how (where, when, who) decisions get taken at the network level

CONFLICT RESOLUTION: how conflicts are resolved effectively

INFORMATION PROCESSING: how information flows among members and is managed

KNOWLEDGE MANAGEMENT: how knowledge is created, captured, shared and used across the network

MOTIVATION: how members are motivated to join/remain within the network

RISK/BENEFIT SHARING: how the risks and rewards are allocated across members of the network

COORDINATION: how the operations of the network are integrated and coordinated

KEY PROCESSES IN NETWORK MANAGEMENT

The final stage of our ecosystem building is the 'performing' part. How do we get the various entities aligned such that they deliver emergent properties?

Let's begin with the 'finding' challenge. And here we need to be clear about what elements we have to assemble. What makes up a viable ecosystem; what's in a Value Network?

We can unpack this a little and look at the roles in more detail. They fall into three broad categories: what we call 'Bookends', 'Movers' and 'Shapers'.

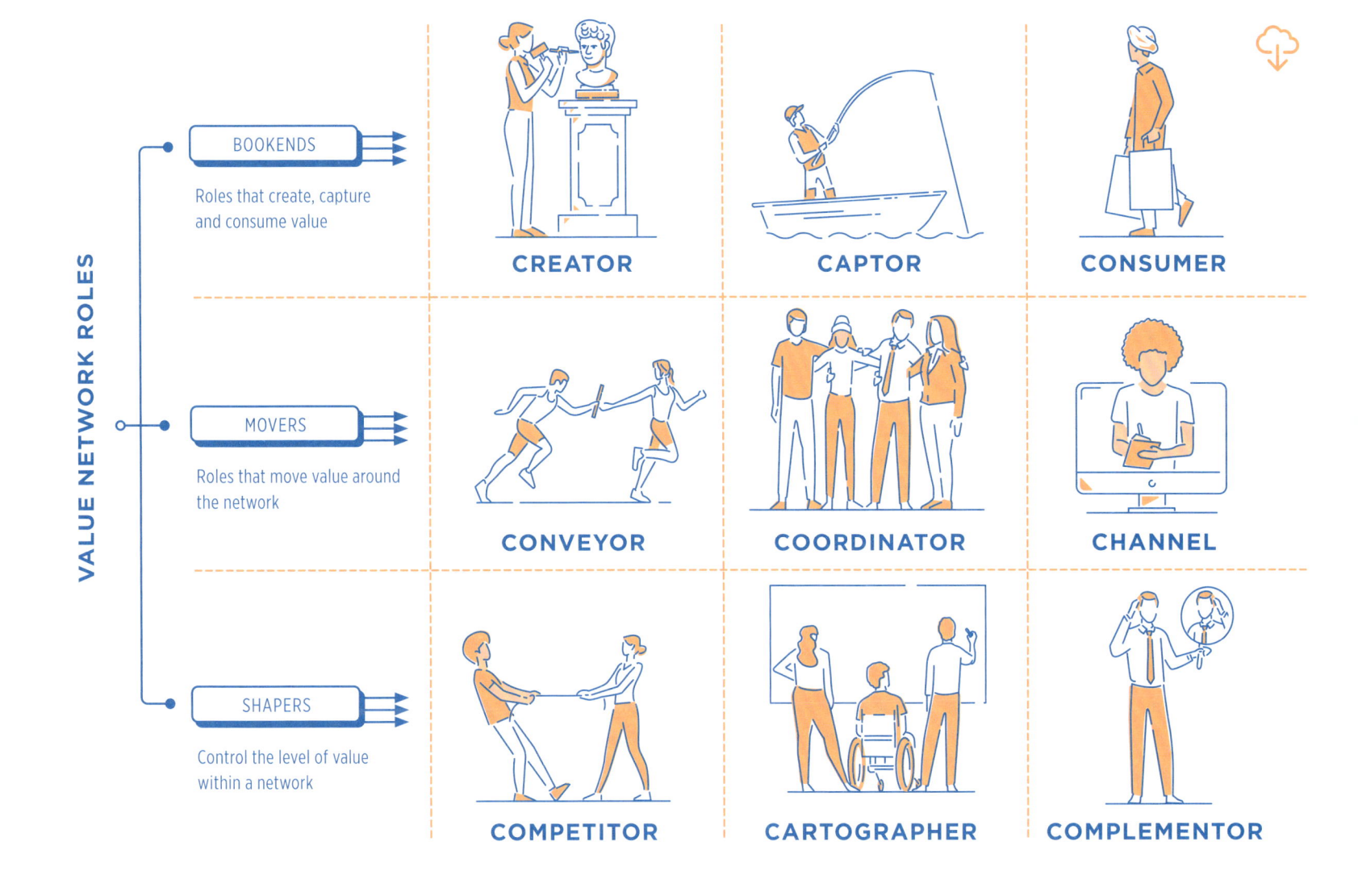

CHAP IV — CONFIGURING VALUE NETWORKS

VALUE NETWORK ROLES

BOOKENDS
Roles that create, capture and consume value

- **CREATOR**
- **CAPTOR**
- **CONSUMER**

MOVERS
Roles that move value around the network

- **CONVEYOR**
- **COORDINATOR**
- **CHANNEL**

SHAPERS
Control the level of value within a network

- **COMPETITOR**
- **CARTOGRAPHER**
- **COMPLEMENTOR**

BOOKENDS

VALUE CREATORS, CAPTORS, AND CONSUMERS

Bookends are the roles at the start and end of the value journey; the roles that create, capture and consume value. In a simplified example we might create a wonderful ice cream which our end user enjoys on a hot summer's day. We create something of value and receive an indication of how much our user values it by the money they pay us, and by seeing the happy smiles on their faces.

The reality is often not quite so simple. Our market may consist of a family in which parents buy their children an ice cream as a treat. The children have the enjoyable – valuable – experience of eating the ice cream, but the parents also have value in the form of some peace and quiet for a few minutes.

Our ability to create value depends on being able to reach our market. We may have to pay a proportion of our sales receipts to the park owner who rents us the concession – so they also capture some value from the process. As do the ingredient suppliers who sell us the materials we need to make our ice cream. And so on.

What appears a simple transaction is in fact a lot more complex and we need to understand and align the different interests in the process. In particular we need to think about three complementary roles.

VALUE CONSUMPTION IS SOMETIMES MULTI-LAYERED – THERE ARE DIFFERENT LEVELS AND THOSE WHO PROCURE OR PURCHASE MAY NOT BE THE FINAL END USER.

VALUE CREATORS

CATEGORY ⟶ BOOKENDS

[Definition › Creating new value in the innovation process]

Value Creators are those who develop new value – the innovators. This can be one organisation, a partnership or joint venture, or it can be done across a distributed network. The key aspect of this creation is that it is new value.

Think about what goes into creating the value of watching a movie. It's not the product of a lone genius, but the outcome of a shared process of value creation; they bring that innovation to life with their ideas. The scriptwriters, of course, but also those who bring complementary skills: the cameramen who understand how to make magic with images, frame shots, explore different perspectives; the sound team, able to work with textures on the audio side, hearing a pin drop, when to use silence; the music, painting with tones, giving dramatic mood; the set designers, laying over the location their magic mixture of props and scenery; the costume designers, bringing an era to life through clothes; and of course the actors who bring it to life, from the stars at the centre to the extras who help give it believability, help the viewer imagine themselves to be a part of it. They are all Value Creators. This is the same with our innovation – the entrepreneur, or intrapreneur, the innovation team, their organisation, key innovation development partners, and even funders and investors are all Value Creators.

As our innovation moves towards scale, there are often significant changes that occur in the area of value creation. The first is that some of the Value Creators we initially needed to collaborate with are no longer necessary. For instance, if our innovation development has been supported through an accelerator or lab, their value creation services may no longer be required. Or if we have developed the innovation within a university research lab, then we're likely to change the nature

ACTIVITY

Think of examples of Value Creators in innovations you know of.

of our partnership with the university as we move towards commercialisation.

Second, scaling often brings with it significant strains on our cash flow for a number of reasons. One of the most common is that as we aim to meet demand, our costs are likely to increase faster than our revenue. Therefore, this is often a time when new Value Creators, in the form of investors, are needed. They'll come on board, but only if there is something in it for them, such as a share in the business or some other benefit.

INNOVATION RELIES ON DIVERSE VALUE CREATORS COLLABORATING FOR NEW SCALABLE SOLUTIONS.

VALUE CONSUMERS

CATEGORY ⟶ BOOKENDS
[Definition › Those who gain value from the use of the innovation]

At the other end of this bookshelf we have the market – those who consume the value which our system creates. These are the players who derive value from the use of our innovation.

Our innovation might be used by individuals, businesses, organisations or governments. For many products and services, those who gain value from it may not directly purchase it – that's often the case with public services like education or health.

CHAP IV — CONFIGURING VALUE NETWORKS

THE RULE OF THUMB IS THAT THE MORE STAKEHOLDERS THAT COMPRISE THE VALUE CONSUMER ROLE, THE MORE COMPLEX SCALING CAN BE.

It's easy to assume a rather simple model of who does the value consuming which focuses on business-to-consumer (B2C) products and services. But this leaves out large parts of the economy, government and society. For such areas we think about potentially three types of Value Consumer: buyers, users and target impact groups.

For B2C markets, the buyer also uses the product and gains the ultimate value from its use. For business-to-business (B2B) markets, the buyer is often separate from the user, but both are often the ultimate Value Consumer through better business operations.

For business-to-government (B2G) and public good markets (e.g., the NHS in the UK), the buyer (procurement teams, budget holders, etc.) is usually different from the user (clinical health workers) who are different from the impact group (the patients who ultimately derive the value of the product or service).

The rule of thumb is that the more stakeholders that comprise the Value Consumer role, the more complex scaling can be.

It is also important to note that Value Consumers are not a passive group; they can impact the value we can capture, such as through online reviews or taking on jobs that we previously performed (e.g., printing out their own boarding passes on a plane). Value Consumers can also help us create value through activities such as engaging in open innovation processes – for example, the toymaker Lego has very successfully recruited its consumers to become co-creators, bringing in their ideas for new models.

VALUE CAPTORS

CATEGORY ⟶ BOOKENDS

[Definition › Capturing value from the development and delivery of the innovation]

VALUE CONSUMERS IN PUBLIC GOODS MARKETS CAN BE BROKEN INTO THREE TYPES – BUYER, USER AND TARGET IMPACT GROUPS.

So far this looks a simple enough story – value being created and consumed. But there's another key role here which is occupied by those who capture value from the innovation not by using it, but by being a part of it. This is the process of extracting value from the Value Network that is not derived directly from the use of the innovation.

CONFIGURING VALUE NETWORKS

This is where the entrepreneur takes their profit from the risks they have taken. It is investors in the company which launches and sells the product or service. And it's all the other supply-side players whose complementary goods and services link together to create the offering.

We need these different players to be part of our Value Network, our ecosystem. But we also need to recognise that they need an incentive – what's in it for them? Importantly this doesn't have to be a financial gain or reward; there are other ways to capture value from the process – for example:

- Learning
- Access to resources
- Access to networks
- Access to customers
- Reputation and social identity

The key message is that we need to think about what motivates our potential partners to join our ecosystem. What benefits can they take from it? What is the value they can capture?

MOVERS

VALUE CHANNELS, CONVEYORS AND COORDINATORS

Let's dig a little deeper into the different roles involved in an ecosystem. Apart from the creators, captors and consumers there are others in the network. And in particular we need to think about 'Movers' – entities that move value around the Value Network. Three roles stand out here: Value Channels, Conveyors and Coordinators.

ACTIVITY

Think of examples of Value Captors in innovations you know of and the value they are seeking to capture.

VALUE CHANNELS

CATEGORY → MOVERS

[Definition › Entities that help you reach your customers without adding value to the innovation]

Channels are passive entities that are used for reaching consumers. For example, the internet offers a channel for sales and order processing. Channels are passive in the sense that, like roads or railways, they exist as infrastructure but are independent of the nature of the traffic using them. They are important, necessary elements in scaling but they are not sufficient to assure scale. If they weren't present or if they are disrupted then value movement couldn't take place, but they are not active elements in the value creation process.

Channels are ways of moving value from either upstream through a supply chain or downstream to a consumer. The value might be in the form of a product or service, or by just increasing consumers' knowledge of the product or service, such as through advertising on a website.

Channels do not add value to the product or service itself. They can increase efficiency, reduce friction and potentially reduce cost, so although this is increasing potential value for the consumer, it is not changing the value derived from the use of the innovation itself. This means that the relationship with them is almost always transactional and they are usually only concerned with financial payment for their service

However, it would be wrong to see channels as just a commodity business that don't have the potential to scale in and of themselves – something which Malcolm McLean, the pioneer of the shipping container revolution, was well aware of (→ 'Success stories' p.17). We'll come back to look at his scaling story in more detail in the next chapter.

Without channels, the Value Network could be incomplete – though the presence of the channel may not be sufficient to ensure widespread adoption of an innovation. Today's → INFLUENCERS do the same via YouTube and Instagram, actively promoting and enabling innovations to reach their intended target market. They carry the message deep into the heart of the early majority segment of the Rogers innovation adoption curve. Also, think about Earl Tupper. He had the channels set up via shops but no one was coming into those stores to buy his product. He needed a new channel (social marketing) but he also needed an activist (Brownie Wise) to help make the connection. She acted in another of our value roles: that of conveyor.

SOMETIMES WE NEED SOME EXTRA HELP TO GET THE MESSAGE ACROSS – THAT'S WHERE 'CONVEYORS' COME IN.

VALUE CONVEYORS

CATEGORY ⟶ MOVERS

[Definition › Active entities that deliver value to you or for you, adding value through the process]

Conveyors are players actively involved in the process of adding value to how our solution comes into being and how it is experienced by consumers. Essentially, the value of the innovation grows through the activities they perform. Conveyors are the backbone of supply chains. They are more than just channels. This can be upstream, such as the manufacturing of core components in a product; for instance, different tiers of suppliers in the car industry. Or it can be downstream, such as a ministry of education deploying edtech solutions in classrooms that rely on the training and the delivery of teachers and classroom assistants for impact.

→ INFLUENCER

'Influencers' are individuals active on social media networks who, as the name suggests, influence the adoption behaviour of others. They are an example of what Rogers would call 'opinion leaders' – people who are respected and credible for a wider population and whose behaviour influences those of their followers.

In their early days, Netflix transitioned from a channel to a conveyor as they created extra value to the product through recommendation algorithms and allowing consumers to hold a DVD as long as they wanted. Gradually they explored how they could build on this conveyor role to become creators, providing the content which their millions of subscribers could consume. (We'll look more closely at their story in the next chapter.)

VALUE COORDINATORS

CATEGORY ⟶ MOVERS

[Definition › Coordinate how value moves across the Value Network]

Coordinators help to make connections and bring different players together to enact value. For example, a department store offers a physical space in which multiple Value Creators can connect with Value Consumers; street markets and large-scale shopping malls offer a similar opportunity.

In large-scale projects such as major construction, a key role is played by the systems integrator. These managing agents may not build anything but take responsibility for coordinating everything to create the final value for the client and for users of the building.

Other examples include those umbrella organisations which work within sectors supporting collaboration across multiple stakeholders, or secretariats which operate in the public and NGO space to effect similar collaboration.

Some organisations can change their position significantly; a good example is Nike which began life as a shoe importer but has ended up as a major fashion business. Their main role is not the production of goods, but in design, marketing and coordinating supply chains.

CONFIGURING VALUE NETWORKS

In the digital space we've become used to seeing the role of the platform business – essentially offering multi-sided coordination amongst different players. Apple, Alibaba, eBay, Uber, Airbnb and Amazon all offer two-sided markets in which Value Creators, app developers or people with something to sell can be connected with consumers who will value that. Their business model is about charging a fee to both sides to cover their costs of making it an effective platform.

CASE STUDY:
DISRUPTING THE FUNDING OF HUMANITARIAN AID; THE EXAMPLE OF COHERE

The Value Network in humanitarian aid is one of vertical integration, with many aid agencies such as Save the Children and the Red Cross raising money in richer countries and implementing projects in disaster-affected countries. In a number of instances these aid agencies will then provide funding to local organisations who deliver the last mile. In essence, traditional aid agencies are playing the role of conveyor, adding value to the monetary donation with their expertise.

As an attempt to disrupt this, a charity called GiveDirectly, a scaling success story of the 2010s, changed the model from adding value to the donations through the provision of services such as health or education projects, to one of channelling the money directly to people living in absolute poverty. GiveDirectly's strategy is one of rejecting the traditional conveyer model of the aid sector, and instead becoming a channel as it moves the cash from donor to recipient.

Another start-up disrupting the traditional conveyor model is Cohere. They have created a platform which cuts out the middlemen of the traditional NGO system. Cohere seeks to reintermediate by matching potential donors with refugee-led organisations (RLOs) on the Reframe platform and in the process provide direct support to RLOs. 'Pooled Funds'' managed by Cohere and by RLOs enable donors to continue funding along thematic lines. The platform can even cut out the middleman of the intermediary fundraising agency by creating pathways for individuals to donate online from anywhere in the world.

The boundaries between channels, coordinators and conveyors can sometimes be blurry. You may not always be able to tell them apart, so we have provided a little cheat sheet.

MOVER CHEAT SHEET

ATTRIBUTE	CONVEYOR	COORDINATOR	CHANNEL
Adds value to the innovation itself	Yes	Sometimes	No
Active or passive	Active	Both/either	Passive
Is either upstream or downstream from the creator	Yes	Both/either	Yes
Coordinates multiple creators and multiple consumers in one place or through one mechanism	No	Yes	No

CONFIGURING VALUE NETWORKS

SHAPERS

VALUE CARTOGRAPHERS, COMPETITORS AND COMPLEMENTORS

The third group of roles are those we call 'Shapers', because they do just that – they shape the potential amount of value that can be created, consumed, moved and captured within a Value Network. They could act as Value Cartographers having regulatory or other authority through which they mark out the pitch and set the rules by which the game is played out. They could be competitors with whom we interact to carve out shares of the playing space. And they could be complementors, not directly involved in our game but able to enhance it in some way from their external perspective.

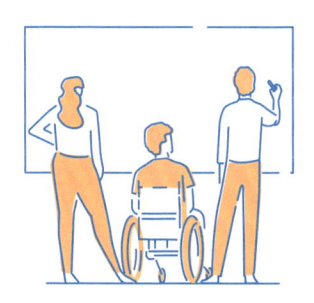

VALUE CARTOGRAPHERS

CATEGORY ⟶ SHAPERS

[Definition › Determine the boundaries and amount of value in a 'market']

Cartographers are the ones who make the maps; they play key roles in structuring a market and determining how much value is possible within a Value Network. Some examples are:

- *Legislatures: creating laws, regulations, policies, investment and tax rules that you will need to adhere to*

- *Courts: interpreting those laws and regulations (e.g., IP law, anti-trust law, contract law, etc.)*

TIP
A good example of cartographers at work is in the regulatory framework which surrounds innovations and which shapes its rate and direction of development – for example in the field of electro-mobility with subsidies for 'green' vehicles and penalties for older fossil-fuel powered ones.

- *Unions: determining how much value is captured by workers vis-à-vis shareholders*

- *Umbrella organisations: industry bodies that create rules, norms and industry-wide incentives*

- *Standards bodies: determining key technical standards that must be met*

- *Consumer rights organisations: influencing laws and behaviour through advocacy and litigation*

- *State ministries and institutions: market making as investors (Value Creators), policy makers and often as large-scale consumers*

Cartographers can play a major role in accelerating – or slowing – the journey to scale. Think about the current moves towards scaling electromobility; much of the journey to scale will be influenced by the regulatory roadmap. Policies like subsidies or tax relief on electric vehicles, or those which militate against fossil fuels, will provide acceleration – for example, at the time of writing the UK has a target of no new cars running only on fossil fuels by 2030. Equally, legislation to ensure compliance can slow down scaling possibilities – think about the EU's stance on genetically modified organisms which has acted as a brake on investment and exploration of this technology.

The power of cartography is also clear in establishing norms which help (or hinder) scale. Government procurement rules across Europe were a key factor in the rapid scaling of adoption of quality standards around the → ISO 9000 MODEL. Put simply, only suppliers who were certified could bid for government contracts – effectively shaping a market which pulled organisations towards adoption of ISO 9002.

It's not just governments; many other bodies act as cartographers. For example, World Health Organization (WHO) approval and International Federation of Pharmaceutical Manufacturers and Associations (IFPMA) pressure will have a significant impact on the scaling of a new drug determining if they can get it onto the WHO's essential medicines list. The National Institute for Health and Care Excellence (NICE) plays a similar role in the UK's public procurement advice around medical supplies.

→ ISO 9000

The International Standards Organization (ISO) published a series of standards (ISO9000 family) relating to quality management within organisations. It became a powerful normative force because organisations needed to demonstrate they were certified as complying with these standards if they wished to act as suppliers to a wide variety of public and private sector organisations.

CONFIGURING VALUE NETWORKS

Trade unions are another source of potential cartographic influence; their role in shaping the speed and direction of adoption to scale can be seen in many innovations – for example the adoption of digital printing technologies or current negotiations around changing levels of automation, the use of drones and the deployment of AI solutions in the transport sector.

One important aspect of the cartography role is that it encourages active attempts to recruit cartographers and to influence their decision making. Lobbying is big business and translates to attempts to persuade or otherwise influence the process of map-making. Not for nothing do organisations commit some of their brightest minds to spend days sitting in meetings of standards committees to help shape the future maps around key innovation areas.

MOBILE BANKING

By 2020, Revolut had become a darling of the UK fintech sector. Since its foundation in 2015 it has scaled dramatically, attracting over 15 million customers by February 2021. However, it is a newcomer when it comes to fintech innovation and still lags way behind one of the original leaders in mobile money, M-PESA, which was started by Safaricom in Kenya in 2007 and now has over 50 million customers.

Why was Silicon Savannah – the technology ecosystem in Kenya – able to gain an almost 10-year head start on the global financial centre of London in producing scalable mobile money solutions? Cartographers.

London had an established financial centre with significant influence on UK regulatory decisions. Kenya had less financial institution influence on regulation, and in fact, the Central Bank of Kenya (CBK) played a significant role in supporting M-PESA to take off, including quickly agreeing to insure deposits. The CBK as a proactive cartographer enabled M-PESA to lead the way in mobile money.

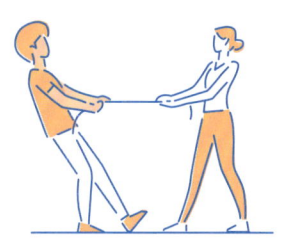

VALUE COMPETITORS

CATEGORY ⟶ SHAPERS

[Definition › Stakeholders with similar value offerings for the same groups, or that rival you for resources]

Value consumption involves consumers choosing amongst options – what we term 'Value Competitors'. Back to our ice-cream analogy: We might find ourselves competing in the park against other ice-cream sellers, or those offering fruit juices or candy. They are all targeting our potential consumers with alternative value offerings.

The general rule is that the more competitors we have, the less value will be able to be created by individual competitors and in that market as a whole.

We see different types of competitors that innovations face when scaling:

- *Direct competition: Similar products and services for the same Value Consumers – e.g., Betamax vs. VHS, Android vs. iOS, Deliveroo vs. Uber Eats*

- *Indirect competitors: Different products or services that can be seen as substitutes by Value Consumers – e.g., cinema vs. bowling, bike vs. taxi, library vs. Google*

- *Business as usual: One of the biggest challenges for new innovations and ventures is inertia and vested interests*

- *Resource competition: Competition for scarce resources, investment and skilled staff*

- *Value Network competition: Competitors for entities playing other roles than Value Consumers, such as co-creators, conveyors and cartographers*

TIP

The impact of competition is usefully explored in the book.

Kim, W.C. & Mauborgne, R. (2015). Blue Ocean Strategy, Expanded Edition: How to Create Uncontested Market Space and Make the Competition Irrelevant. Brighton MA: Harvard Business Review.

IV CONFIGURING VALUE NETWORKS

The important thing is that these competitors all shape the context in which value creation/consumption can take place. So, we need to be clear who/what our competitors are and explore ways of minimising their influence, which might include finding ways to work with them in so-called ➜ 'CO-OPETITION'.

WHAT ELSE – AND WHO ELSE – DO WE NEED TO HELP UNLOCK THE VALUE IN OUR INNOVATION?

VALUE COMPLEMENTORS

CATEGORY ⟶ SHAPERS

[Definition › Entities and stakeholders that influence the value of your innovation through their products, services and actions]

Value Complementors do just that – they complement the value an innovation offers. Sometimes they are essential: Thomas Edison's attempts to revolutionise domestic lighting arrangements depended on having something (an electricity supply) into which users could plug his new light bulb innovation.

An important aspect of Value Complementors is that we do not directly own or control them. Edison's early problems (captured well in the movie "The Current War")

➜ **CO-OPETITION**
The phenomenon of collaboration between competitors.

were around who controlled the electricity supply and the system (alternating or direct current) on which it operated. Whichever way that standards battle went, the successful scaling of his lighting innovation would depend on these complementors.

That's the pattern today: In an increasingly interconnected world, Value Networks contain symbiotic relationships with entities that they do not have partnerships with. For example, Bluetooth devices require other devices to contain Bluetooth to deliver any value. SodaStream requires access to potable water.

Innovations often fail to scale because of the lack of such infrastructure or the slow speed with which it emerges. The Better Place problem was classic network failure – the idea depended on having complementors in place which weren't ready.

The Netflix model with which we are now very familiar would not have been possible without the early (and illegal) experiments around file-sharing and torrent technologies which allowed widespread diffusion across social media platforms. Before that, Netflix depended on physical DVD rentals, with geographical limits on their reach as a consequence. Streaming was a big complementor to their growth.

Complementors may also emerge as surprises. The pace of innovation, particularly in the digital world, has meant that there are key shifts in the number and combinations of layers of innovation that can suddenly unlock game-changing innovations. For example, cloud computing provides the engine on which so many platform businesses now depend.

Complementors come in different shapes and sizes. They can be an entity that is a piece of physical or digital infrastructure; they can be former competitors or part-time competitors (co-opetition); they can be producing goods or services that your innovation relies on or leverages.

TIP
Concern about the rate of adoption of electric vehicles (= a scaling problem) is strongly focused around the lack of sufficient charging infrastructure. This article by McKinsey & Co. captures the problem well:

CONFIGURING VALUE NETWORKS

Some examples include:

- Sport and beer
- Internet access and internet-enabled devices
- Logistics and strong public infrastructure
- Services around an event e.g., travel – hotels, planes, car hire, travel insurance
- Telecommunications companies and mobile money
- Cold storage and vaccines
- Universities and professions

SOMETIMES IT'S A CASE OF THE 'RIGHT IDEA, WRONG TIME' PROBLEM – WITHOUT COMPLEMENTORS EVEN THE BEST SOLUTIONS MAY FAIL.

A COMPLEMENTOR STORY

Brainboxes, an ➜ Internet of Things (IoT) hardware and software company, saw the potential of the Bluetooth early, creating their first Bluetooth-enabled devices in 1999. But most of the market wasn't ready – they needed the big players to bring out Bluetooth in their devices, and the big players were dragging their feet.

Brainboxes were right about the investment, but they had significant problems due to the timing. Being amongst the first to market with a Bluetooth device whose purpose is to connect with other Bluetooth-enabled devices isn't the best position to be in, because there is no value to consumers if none of the other devices they want to connect to have Bluetooth. For Brainboxes they managed to survive this 'early mover disadvantage' by spreading their bets across 7 devices (2 of which were a success). Without this approach they would have fallen foul of Marc Andreessen the tech entrepreneur and investor's maxim that "being early is the same as being wrong."

➜ **THE INTERNET OF THINGS (IOT)**

refers to the fact that it is now possible to put intelligent devices embedded in many pieces of equipment and able to communicate with each other. An example would be a 'smart home' in which the various pieces of technology – domestic appliances, communication and entrainment systems, heating and ventilation, etc., would all be able to communicate with each other.

It's worth thinking about ways of working with complementors to leverage ecosystem benefits in scaling. Two particular examples illustrate this. The first involves what we call 'layering'. Complementors often provide a base on which new innovations and enterprises can stand on the shoulders of giants. Zoom and Netflix have both been successful innovations because they anticipated and leveraged the roll out of fast internet speeds which would enable them to piggyback this technology to deliver their services.

Many innovations create value, not just through their direct use, but also by creating the foundation for other innovations and businesses to develop around them. For example, Airbnb has created a whole slew of associated cleaning and property management enterprises solely focused on supporting Airbnb hosts. These businesses are not connected to Airbnb, but they are in a symbiotic dance. Their existence makes Airbnb more attractive as an option for potential hosts, increasing the value creation potential of Airbnb for hosts whilst creating a new subsector of the property management and cleaning sectors.

→ 'STITCHING' is similar to layering, but instead of building on other innovations it involves combining different innovations and businesses together to create something new. For example the revolution in dealing with childhood polio depended on stitching (see box on cold chain miracles).

→ **STITCHING**
We call this stitching as an acknowledgement of Sarasvathy's concept of 'crazy quilts', the stitching together of different partners, as part of her effectuation theory of entrepreneurship. For us, stitching goes beyond partners, and combines complementors, businesses, technologies, as well as new behaviours and norms.

COLD CHAIN MIRACLES

The world is on the threshold of eradicating polio. It has been able to reach this point due to innovations in different areas, as pointed out in Tim Harford's book *Fifty Things that Made the Modern Economy*. Children wouldn't have been successfully vaccinated against polio without the stitching together of innovations: shipping containers for efficient transportation; refrigeration to keep the vaccines at the cold temperature needed in a cold chain; barcodes to make tracking individual shipments down to the vial level easy.

It is only by combining and leveraging these three innovations (amongst others), that the value created by vaccines can be fully realised by individuals and whole societies.

MIND THE GAP: THE IMPACT OF INCOMPLETE VALUE NETWORKS

In the aftermath of the first wave of Covid-19 in 2020, Ian carried out research on the role of → MAKER TECHNOLOGIES and localised additive manufacturing on plugging the hole in PPE supply chains. In many ways it was research about a breakthrough moment for distributed small-scale manufacturing, with PPE being developed and manufactured by small → MAKERSPACES the world over. The most striking example was the M19 Collective in India who manufactured over 1 million articles of PPE in less than 50 days.

However, the potential value creation of makerspaces creating PPE was not scaled and maximised as it could have been. In interviews with makers, the problem of a missing complementor consistently appeared. Unlike in the field of software with GitHub, there was no globally recognised central repository for designs. Designs that were proving successful in one location could not be easily accessed by others in other locations. There were different sites that did have some PPE designs, but they weren't well known enough or structured in a way that worked for other makers.

We cannot quantify how many more PPE items could have been produced if there had been such a well-known central repository, but we know that it would have reduced much wasted trial and error in different parts of the globe and created huge lifesaving value. «

CHAPTER IV — SUMMARY
WHAT YOU HAVE LEARNED IN THIS CHAPTER

▷ A Value Network is primarily made up of three categories: Bookends, Movers and Shapers, each containing three roles that different entities can play.

▷ Bookends are Value Creators, Consumers and Captors.

▷ Movers are Value Channels, Conveyors and Coordinators.

▷ Shapers are Value Cartographers, Competitors and Complementors.

→ **MAKER TECHNOLOGY**
Maker technologies is a phrase used to describe tools and methods such as electronics, robotics, 3D printing, metalworking, woodworking, laser cutting, extruding and others that are used in small scale manufacturing, often in makerspaces.

→ **MAKERSPACE**
"Makerspaces are places where people can come together to create or invent things, either using traditional crafts or technology." Definition of 'makerspace' from the Cambridge Advanced Learner's Dictionary & Thesaurus (2023).

CHAP V
WORKING WITH VALUE ROLES: MANAGING OUR NETWORK

This chapter explores the ways in which we might work with the different value roles described in Chapter 4. In particular it looks at the ways in which roles can change over time and the concept of inner and outer Value Networks over which we have differing degrees of influence in configuring our networks.

Mapping the Value Network is a key step in scaling – making sure we are aware of all the different players and roles which are needed to help us create and capture value from our solution. But let's go back to our core model of building and managing an ecosystem. We need all of the entities described in the previous chapter, but we don't or can't control them all. Even Henry Ford with his massively vertically integrated system couldn't control everything. His fast-growing company ran aground and nearly sank in the early 1920s because of challenges around Value Competitors (players like General Motors were offering much more choice to an increasingly segmented market).

We need to understand the different entities involved in a Value Network and then work out how they might be configured and managed in strategic fashion; that's the 'performing' part of our finding, forming, performing model.

NINE KEY ROLES IN VALUE NETWORKS

CREATOR · CAPTOR · CONSUMER
CONVEYOR · COORDINATOR · CHANNEL
COMPETITOR · CARTOGRAPHER · COMPLEMENTOR

But that's not as easy as it looks – any more than riding a horse is as simple as jumping on its back. There's a lot we need to take into account. For example: individual entities can play multiple roles at once. Too often we think of each stakeholder playing a single role and are blinded to the other potential roles they can play, and where their roles can actually be in contradiction to each other. Entities roles can also change over time, particularly over the different stages of the innovation journey.

Because entities can play different roles at once, and potentially across time, Value Networks are dynamic. They are continually changing, creating both opportunities and threats.

As we'll see shortly, there are parts of our network we can exert control over (our inner Value Network) and other parts where we have little or no direct influence (our outer Value Network).

MULTIPLE ROLES AT ONCE

Actors in a Value Network can play many different roles; the lines between role types can often be blurred and this opens up opportunities for different forms of relationship-making.

Value Creators rarely do this purely for philanthropic motives: they are looking to become Value Captors as well. Creators may also play a role as consumers – for example by working on their internal processes and then using what they have learned to create a value offering. This was the case with → SLACK, which began life as an internal platform for communicating about their (not very successful) online gaming business. They realised that this suite of tools had value externally – and the rest is history.

Lego, for example, has pursued a strategy of increasingly open innovation for several years by working alongside their key customers (Value Consumers) in co-creation activities like Lego Factory and *Lego Ideas*. Such partnerships bring Value Consumers into the game as Value Creators and Value Captors, sharing royalties and non-financial rewards like recognition.

→ **SLACK**

Slack is a communications and workflow app which is widely used in professional and organisational communication as well as a community platform.

LEGO CASE STUDY

When Lego was in trouble and needed a turnaround, they didn't look inward for solutions, they embraced their customers. Lego needed ideas, so they engaged their customers, not just in user-centred design practices of consultation but also in full-scale open innovation by launching Lego Ideas, an online crowd-sourcing platform providing a space for consumers to submit ideas and also select ideas through voting for them.

Their strategy was to turn Value Consumers into Value Creators, espousing their philosophy that "people don't have to work for us to work with us."

FIVE CASE STUDIES ON INNOVATION AT LEGO

Overview and history of innovation at Lego

Explores how Lego opened up its Value Network to co-creators

Looks at the long-term development of Lego's innovation approach

Offers some examples of co-creation with users at Lego

Explores the challenges and opportunities of co-creation across a Value Network

CASE STUDY ON THREADLESS

The example of giffgaff (which we'll look at in the next chapter) is similar: they have carved out a special niche in the highly competitive mobile phone market by engaging with customers as creators; in this instance as technical support provided on a peer-to-peer helping community model. The customer user group is also acting here as a conveyor, helping strengthen the after-sales support service offering for giffgaff.

Many online businesses – see, for example, *Threadless* – have moved to scale by engaging with user communities and creating a sense of co-creation.

INNOVATION IS INCREASINGLY MOVING TO A WORLD OF CO-CREATION ACROSS COMMUNITIES.

ROLES CHANGE OVER TIME

Value Networks are by no means fixed – they change over time. For example, those who were Value Creators originally may change roles. Nike moved from being a value creator directly designing and importing shoes to increasing its presence and reach as a coordinator, operating a platform across which it leveraged its brand through an elaborate arrangement of subcontracts and partnerships around the value creation side of things. And, of course, one-time partners in value creation may fall out and end up as competitors. What we often see is that over time players add to the roles they play and in doing so strengthen their hand. Brownie Wise began as a very successful conveyor; she then codified her own experience into a model which others could follow, building up her teams of social marketers across the country. Finally she created the platform which sat at the heart of the Tupperware business, linking conveyors with consumers who, in time, might also become conveyors. She worked tirelessly to extend the social marketing platform, providing training via newsletters and training manuals, and building a community of practice with motivational and skills benefits. (In fact she anticipated YouTube by over fifty years, making a 52 minute TV film (*A Tupperware Home Party*) as a training tool!) She was also able to offer her platform to other Value Creators beyond the Tupperware world. She became a coordinator.

In similar fashion, Jeff Bezos took Amazon from being a conveyor, by actively promoting across the passive internet channel the possibilities in bookselling. In particular he helped creators of less popular and niche books to match with consumers with such esoteric interests – exploiting the → *long tail* possibilities that an internet channel and a virtual warehouse model could offer. But then he began adding other elements to the nascent platform: moving into other retail sectors like homeware, electronics and food, creating a platform as a coordinator. And he deepened the channel's potential by creating Amazon Web Services (AWS) which provided a powerful robust service which others could also make use of, taking on a complementor role. He set up Amazon's own-label creation possibilities alongside those of others which his platform marketed – a model which saw the emergence of Amazon as another content creator following in the footsteps of Netflix. (Interestingly Netflix is one of AWS's biggest customers; the Netflix streaming operation depends on Amazon's platform to operate!)

Being aware of the potential for such movement is important in managing at the ecosystem level; there may be new relationships which need to be forged or it may no longer be necessary to keep some players in the network.

Think of it as a dynamic game in which different pieces are moved across the board to create strategic advantage for themselves. Being able to anticipate such moves can help target where new or different relationships need to be formed.

Some examples of potential moves will help illustrate this.

→ **LONG TAIL**
The 'long tail' refers to the fact that for many products and services there is a concentration of high demand followed by a long tail of low demand. Take bookselling for example; there are best-sellers which sell in their millions but a much larger number of books whose market can be measured in very small numbers. For more on this see Anderson, C. (2006). *The Long Tail: Why the Future of Business Is Selling Less of More*. New York: Hyperion.

VALUE ROLE SHIFT EXAMPLES

CREATORS BECOMING CONVEYORS

In traditional value chain thinking, this would be vertical integration to either become involved in the production of the innovations components upstream or to become involved in the distribution of their innovation downstream.

CREATORS BECOMING CARTOGRAPHERS

This can be by joining key industry bodies or government task forces. This goes beyond the role of lobbying and influencing because the creators are now involved in the policy- or law-making process.

CREATORS BECOMING CONSUMERS

During the process of creating an online game, Slack created a workflow and communications application. When the game they were creating failed to take off, they pivoted to commercialising the product that they had created for themselves.

CHANNELS BECOMING CAPTORS

Channels require value capture to be a viable business – players like UPS and DHL have turned delivery into extremely profitable businesses.

CHANNELS BECOMING CONVEYORS

Netflix started out as barely more than a channel, posting DVDs to Value Consumers. However, it managed to add value by allowing consumers to keep the DVDs for as long as they liked and used an algorithm to improve search.

CHANNELS BECOMING COORDINATORS

Amazon started as a channel, similar to Netflix, but instead of posting videos, they sold books online. They quickly expanded from a book seller to a marketplace, bringing customers and sellers together onto the world's biggest platform.

WORKING WITH VALUE ROLES: MANAGING OUR NETWORK

CHANNELS BECOMING COMPETITORS

The rise in the white labelling of products has seen a number of channels in the retail space start competing with creators who are using them by carrying their own brand versions of the same products.

CONVEYORS BECOMING CREATORS

Conveyors by definition are creating value, but to someone else's innovation. They can also move directly into the creator space by moving up or down the supply chain to become the main creator of a product or service. Netflix, again, is an example of this, where they have moved from being a content streamer to a content producer.

COORDINATOR TO CREATOR TO COMPETITOR

Department stores are coordinators because they house concessions – almost like mini-shops for different brands – thereby coordinating Value Creators with Value Consumers. However, they also use white labelling to create their own products that are sold as their own products, competing with the other brands they stock.

COORDINATOR TO CARTOGRAPHER

Coordinators often have significant power over the market, either indirectly through setting standards for industries, or through significant lobbying power with legislators. This means that coordinators often play the role of cartographer, either directly or indirectly. This is particularly the case in self-regulating markets, where the umbrella organisation sets the rules, e.g., the English Premier League in football.

COORDINATOR TO COMPLEMENTOR

Often coordinators will bundle complementor products and services together. For example, airlines will bundle complementors of flight, hotel, travel insurance and car hire together as offers during the purchasing process.

CHOOSING A CONVEYOR
SOUNDER GOLF

Sounder Golf is a challenger brand that is part of the democratisation of golf movement and aims to bring in a more casual and trendy style of golf clothing and accessories. As a start-up they needed a conveyer who could produce small batches of their high-quality apparel. This led them to choose a manufacturer in Portugal. However, as they started to scale, they needed larger batch runs and they needed resilience in their upstream conveyers. To do this they retained their Portuguese manufacturer and then found another conveyor in India who could produce at larger volumes.

A key decision for them in this process was to ensure that they not only had aligned values on ESG (Environmental, Social and Governance) with the Indian manufacturer, but that they also had a passion for golf. They managed to do this when they found a company whose owner played golf every morning before hitting the office.

MANAGING OUR VALUE NETWORK

An effective ecosystem isn't just having the right players – it also depends on developing strong and supportive working relationships with them. This is the 'forming' part of our model. To do this we need to look a little more closely at our Value Network and explore the Inner Value Network (IVN) with whom we have to have formal and positive relationships and the wider Outer Value Network (OVN) which represents players in the system who we may or may not need to recruit as formal partners.

VALUE NETWORK STRUCTURE

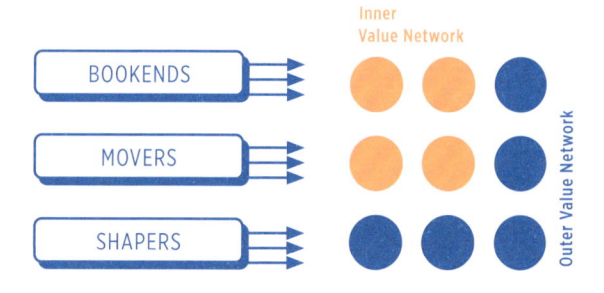

BOOKENDS

MOVERS

SHAPERS

Inner Value Network

Outer Value Network

WORKING WITH VALUE ROLES: MANAGING OUR NETWORK

Back to our horse-riding analogy: if we are trying to ride a number of horses simultaneously, we can't sit on all of them holding the reins; there'll be some with whom we have close contact and others who are at the edge of the herd and we need to find different ways of communicating with and working with them.

Inner Value Network

These are stakeholders and entities that we need some form of agreement with. It can be formal like a contract, or informal like a handshake; but it is the group of entities that we need to interact with to enable our innovation to create value. In the early stages of the innovation journey our IVN will start out with stakeholders who fulfil Bookend roles and at least one of the Mover roles.

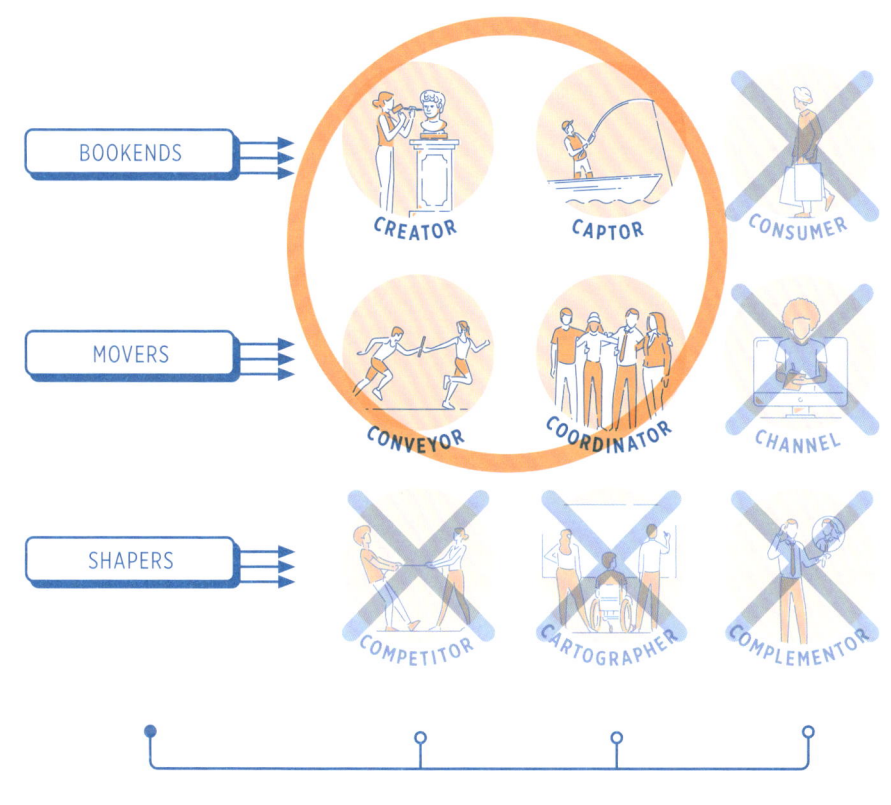

SOME ROLES ARE MORE COMMONLY IVN
INNER VALUE NETWORK

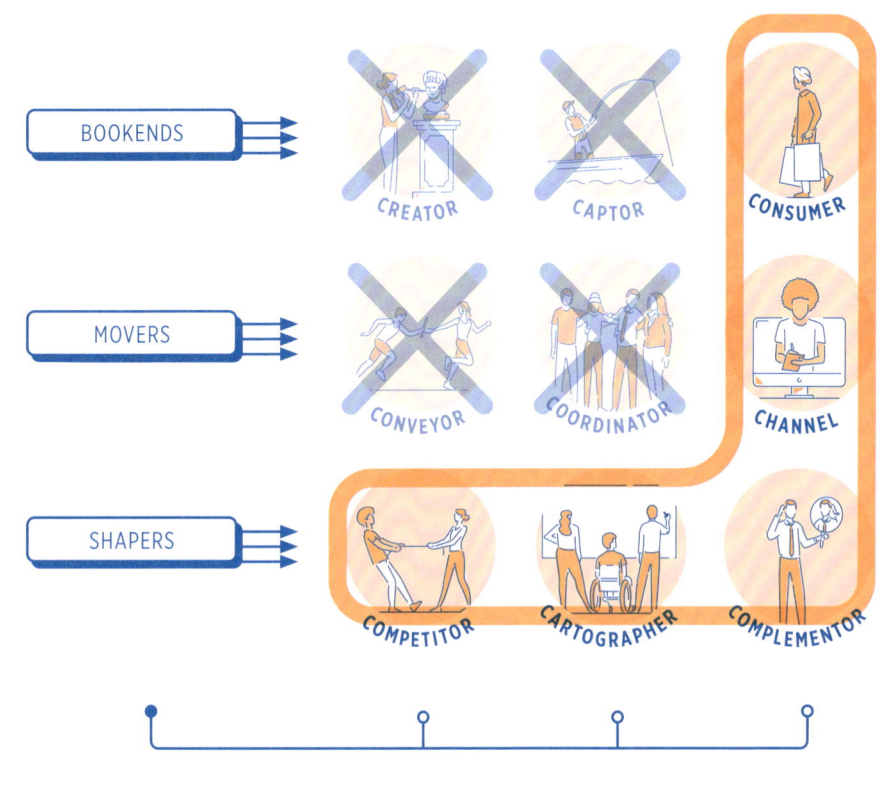

100　PART 1　PREPARING FOR THE SCALING EXPEDITION

BOOKENDS →

- CREATOR ✗
- CAPTOR ✗
- CONSUMER

MOVERS →

- CONVEYOR ✗
- COORDINATOR ✗
- CHANNEL

SHAPERS →

- COMPETITOR
- CARTOGRAPHER
- COMPLEMENTOR

AND SOME ARE MORE COMMONLY OVN
OUTER VALUE NETWORK

Outer Value Network

The Outer Value Network has a huge impact on the value our innovation creates, but we may not have any real relationship with entities in our OVN. Remember, each stakeholder can have multiple roles. Here the big question is around how far we can or should build or create relationships to bring these OVN players into our ecosystem in an active fashion – for example by partnering with consumers as co-creators or working alongside Value Complementors.

Participating in standard-setting groups or engaging in lobbying can help secure relationship advantages amongst cartographers. And co-opetition can also help – not in the sense of building a cartel but rather finding ways to co-exist. As we mentioned earlier, Netflix uses Amazon Web Services to provide the core streaming infrastructure for its offerings which actually compete with Amazon Prime Video's services. Apple uses Samsung components in its smartphones despite the two being direct competitors in the consumer marketplace.

We'll explore tools and techniques for working with Value Networks in the second part of the book.   «

CHAPTER V — SUMMARY
WHAT YOU HAVE LEARNED IN THIS CHAPTER

▷ Entities in the Value Network can and do play multiple roles at once, and these roles change over the scaling journey.

▷ A Value Network has an Inner Value Network (IVN) which consists of entities that the organisation has some formal relationship with, and an Outer Value Network (OVN) with entities that have an effect on the amount of value that can be realised.

▷ As a rule of thumb, the more you scale, the more entities are brought into your IVN.

CHAP VI
SCALE STORIES

This chapter presents some more detailed examples of organisations which have moved innovation to scale, and maps them to the nine roles in our Value Network model. Understanding the way value is built through building a viable ecosystem is key and analysing the different roles being played can help with the finding, forming and performing challenge.

THE MANY SCALING ROUTES

WALKING THE TIGHTROPE

The year was 2006 and all was quiet on the music front – at least for a while. Ever since Shawn Fanning and Sean Parker set up the peer-to-peer (P2P) file-sharing site Napster in 1999, the music industry had struggled to cope with a seismic shift in the way its potential market behaved. Instead of consuming what the big music companies decided was good for them, people had turned to taking what they wanted illegally. As if a piracy virus had spread across the planet, millions were opening up their personal music collections and sharing files with each other across the internet. Napster and a handful of other sites like Gnutella and LimeWire provided the infrastructure, making it easy for people to find and download the music they wanted. For a while it challenged the core of the music industry's business model before the collective legal might of the industry giants reasserted itself. Napster and other sites were pursued by injunctions and strong threats and eventually the flare of illegal file sharing began to sputter. Even Kazaa, which had taken over Napster's mantle, was struggling*.

* **MAKING MUSICAL CONNECTIONS**
You can find a detailed account of the MP3 story in this article: *An Innovation Birthday Card*.

Not that Daniel Ek and Martin Lorentzon saw it that way, sitting around Ek's Stockholm apartment and brainstorming ideas for a new venture. They did this to a backdrop of music playing from Ek's old PC and were both frustrated at the limited range of content they could access (at least legally) and with the delivery experience. They began to see the music not as a background tool to help them think but the core of an experience they thought they might just be able to innovate around.

They had form. In 2006, Ek became a millionaire at age 23 after selling his start-up, Advertigo to Lorentzon's company, Tradedoubler. Their brainstorming quickly took them in a different direction: setting up their own file-sharing system. It was already clear that, quite apart from the difficulties of running a technically illegal system with the threat of being hounded like Napster, the actual operating model of the pirate sector was full of problems: it relied on algorithms which sliced up different pieces of a song held on different people's computers and then transmitted them in fragments which could then be reassembled into a song at the destination point. The management of this complex information traffic flow was enormously difficult and prone to errors and gaps. Quality varied widely; downloads were often incomplete – and all the while people were exposing their computers to payloads which had been attached to the core message by hackers, making it a malware and virus paradise.

Ek and Lorentzon were convinced there was a better way – and that people would be happy to pay for it. They assumed there hadn't been a sudden morality crisis: people had become pirates because the existing music industry wasn't giving them what they wanted; they would value something which legally gave them the same kind of enormous choice but at the quality levels they would like to see.

Part of that model had been demonstrated by the success of iTunes and other music distribution systems. Steve Jobs's great innovation in opening up the MP3 iPod market had not been in the wonderful device on which the music could be played, but in doing the complex background deals with the record companies to enable legal distribution of digital media. It gave consumers some of what they wanted – for example being able to pick and choose the individual tracks they wanted – but at a price; iTunes cost around $2 per track – not exactly cheap.

As they kicked ideas around, another radical thought came up: what the P2P revolution had highlighted was a

TIP
There's an excellent documentary series *(The Playlist)* on Netflix which charts Spotify's journey to scale, viewed from several different perspectives.

sharing economy – the idea that you didn't need to own something personally in order to benefit from it. Listening didn't have to be linked to owning; what Ek and Lorentzon began to explore was whether people might change from an ownership model to one in which they simply 'rented' the music they liked – a kind of pay-as-you-go (PAYG) model. Radio, of course, offered a version of this where the bill was paid by advertisers who funded various streams of music to suit different listener groups (country, jazz, etc.). Listeners 'paid' with their attention to the ads, so might it be possible to do something similar with digital music – to introduce a PAYG model funded by advertising? Lots of possibilities and plenty of innovation space if they could get the value proposition clear. And if they could scale the idea to the point where enough people were consuming it, they could make the very small margins into profitable ones.

Spotify began to crystallise from this Petri dish of possibilities. It took them two years to make licensing deals with record companies, and in 2008, Spotify was launched, opening paid subscriptions to everyone. Free accounts were only available by invitation.

Let's look at their journey to scale along a timeline.

SPOTIFY IS A GREAT EXAMPLE OF THE CHALLENGE IN GETTING TO THE 'RIGHT' VALUE PROPOSITION FROM A WHOLE SEA OF POSSIBILITIES.

PART 1   PREPARING FOR THE SCALING EXPEDITION

2006

2008

Spotify launches as a streaming music playback application for computers, available only in some European countries. Revenue model is mainly subscription with limited ad-supported free accounts, but only available by invitation

Despite being formally limited to Europe, some international users are able to access it, including Mark Zuckerberg who posted "Spotify is so good" on his Facebook page

— **CONVEYOR ROLE**

2006

Initial ideas and sketches
— **START-UP MODE**

2010

Releases a desktop music manager, effectively setting Spotify up as competitor to iTunes
— **COMPETITION**

2011

Formally offered in the USA where in its first year it has a six-month trial period for free.
— **COORDINATOR ROLE**

Quickly gains 1 million paying users
— **COMPLEMENTORS**

Announces that the application will diversify by becoming a platform that could host various music-related applications like lists, charts and photos, and also linked in media like *Rolling Stone* magazine, aiming to offer a wide range of users a platform for exploring their musical tastes
— **ENGAGING VALUE CONSUMERS IN A CLOSER RELATIONSHIP**

Introduces multiple extensions and apps to enable users to personalise their experience.

Introduces the Spotify Apps service, making it possible for third-party developers to design apps that can be hosted within the Spotify computer software
— **COORDINATOR, PLAYING PLATFORM ROLE**

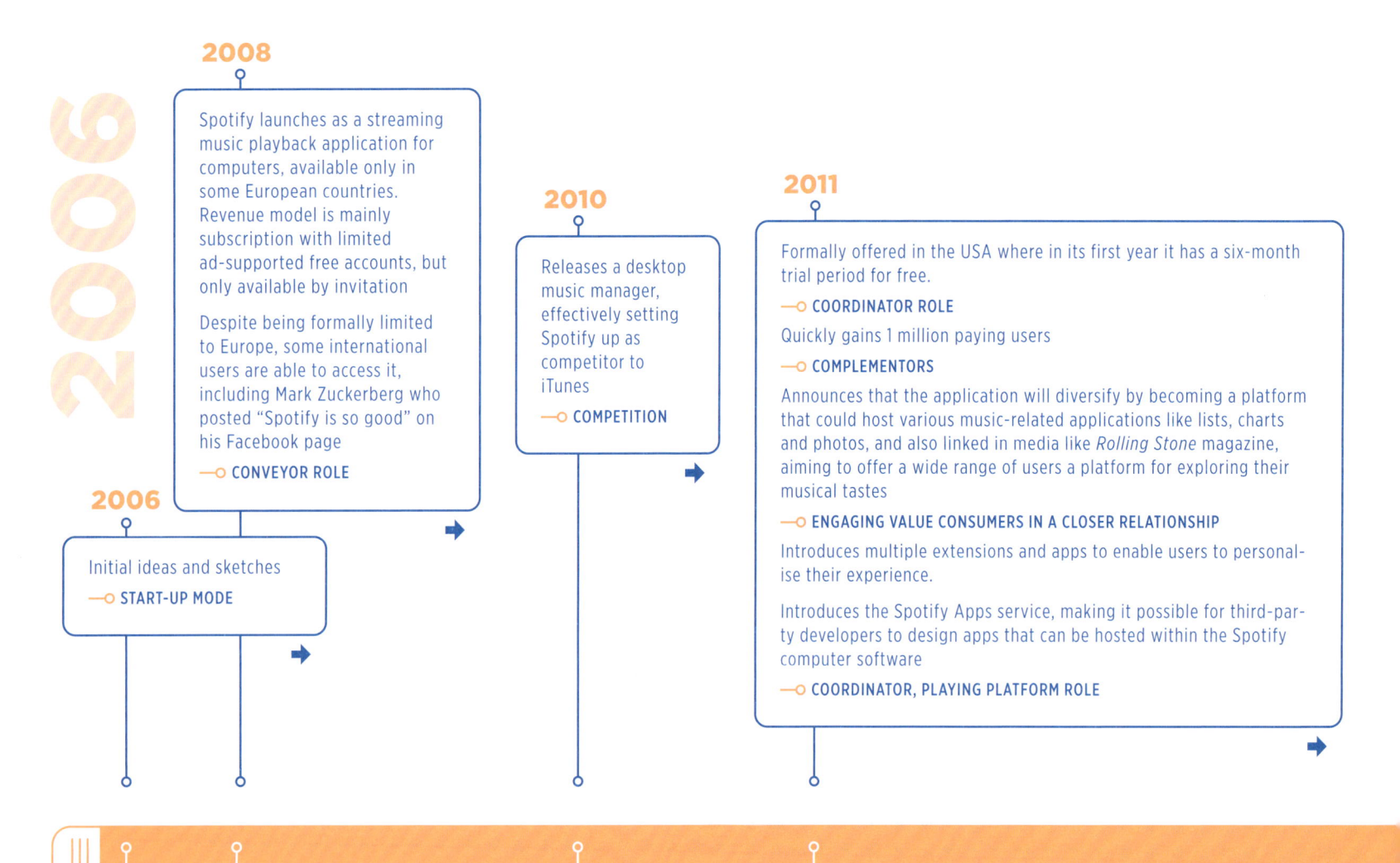

VI SCALE STORIES

2012

Slow to react to mobile phone upsurge, Spotify launches a version for Android. Also introduces Spotify Play Button, an embeddable music player that can be added to websites, blogs or social media profiles to allow visitors to listen to a specific playlist, album or song without leaving the page

2013

Spotify makes its first acquisition when it buys Tunigo, which helps users create, find and share new music and playlists on Spotify

2014

Taylor Swift famously pulls her music from Spotify over concerns about fees, bringing to a head a simmering problem on the content-creation side. Ek's response is to point out that Spotify has paid more than $2 billion to music rights holders since its launch in 2008, arguing that "streaming is better than the piracy as piracy doesn't pay artists a penny"

Continues to create various alliances with social networks such as Facebook, Twitter, Instagram and Snapchat allowing its users to access the app and share its content in various ways, thus improving the user experience

— **VALUE CREATOR PROBLEMS AND RISK AS A NEGATIVE COMPLEMENTOR**

2015

Updates and rebrands itself. Introduces a new home page that will show recommended music, with recommendations improving over time. Launches Discover Weekly, a weekly-generated playlist that gives users two hours of custom-made music recommendations by considering the user's personal taste with their previously enjoyed songs. The company also expands into podcasts, news radio and video streaming, making deals with ESPN, Comedy Central, Vice and the BBC

In June 2015, Spotify announces that the company raised an additional half a billion dollars and had 20 million subscribers out of 75 million listeners

Acquires Seed Scientific, a data science consulting firm

2016

Forms a partnership with music annotation service Genius in 2016, bringing the annotation information from Genius to info cards presented while playing songs on Spotify. They also introduce Release Radar, a personalised playlist that helps users stay up to date on new music releases from artists they usually listen to

Also releases Daily Mix, a series of up to six playlists with near-endless playback, mixing the user's favourite tracks with new and recommended songs

2017

Makes a new deal with Universal Music Group to license its music. Under the deal, some new music will only be available to subscribers for a brief period of time

Taylor Swift returns to Spotify

Introduces Spotify Codes for mobile apps, a way for users to share specific tracks, playlists, artists, or albums with other people

Spotify and Tencent invest in each other, which establishes a strategic partnership with the largest digital service in China

SCALE STORIES

2018

IPO valued at $26.5 billion by the end of the first trading day. Does not issue new shares, but its existing shareholders will take their shares directly to the market. They did not intend to raise capital, but to let investors get their returns

Introduces a new beta feature that gives labels, artists and teams an easier way to submit unreleased music directly to Spotify for playlist consideration

Announces expansion in a total of 13 new countries in the Middle East and North African region. A new Arabic hub is created and several playlists and announcements. Their apps can now support the right-to-left text, suitable for Arabic

—○ VALUE CAPTORS

2019

Car View for Android introduced, allowing devices to have a Now Playing screen when their device is connected to a car's Bluetooth. Also launches the Your Daily Drive custom playlist that replicates the drive time format of most traditional radio stations. This mixes short podcast news updates from NPR, *The Wall Street Journal* and PRI to a mix of user's favourite songs and artists interspersed with songs the listener has yet to discover

—○ INTEGRATES MORE VALUE STREAMS IN THE EXPERIENCE – BECOMING A PLATFORM

2020

Has over 345 million users around the world – there are around 155 million active paid subscriptions for streaming music on this platform

2022

Owns 31% of the worldwide music streaming market, 44% of listeners use the app every day and the average listener listens to more than 40 unique artists every week

More than 50 million songs are now available on Spotify

Continuing and increasingly public debate about the returns to original content creators – estimates suggest it is as low as $0.00318 per stream

THE FUTURE FOR SPOTIFY

Once again we can see the complex interplay as a Value Network is brought together and grown. But we can also see the difficult challenges facing the company as it tries to balance different interests amongst its stakeholders. An early win was getting the support of the music publishers who were the gateway to the content Spotify needed; they converted these players into Value Captors by the simple (but carefully negotiated) device of giving them a revenue stream in the form of royalties. This was a laborious process, taking around two years to conclude. Significantly, Sean Parker, with his considerable experience in Napster's troubled growth, became an early investor (Value Creator and Captor) and provided valuable advice and brokering during this early stage. But the balance is still tilted in favour of this powerful group of music publishers; around 80% of Spotify's catalogue comes from just four major labels.

At the same time, the core of their model is built on giving Value Consumers the pleasurable experience of music – for which they depend on the content creators. Since 2014 and the Taylor Swift battle there has been disquiet that content creators do not receive a fair share of the revenue – particularly as a consequence of the hardships imposed by the Covid-19 pandemic which made live appearances impossible – and that many suffer financial hardship as a result of the shift away from traditional music format sales.

Spotify is *walking a tightrope*, trying to balance these interests and sustain its platform model. It is a precarious position; if popular perception swings further behind the musicians there is a risk that there will be a negative complementor backlash and Value Consumers (and importantly advertisers) may shift away from Spotify. This reflects the constant negotiations that need to happen regarding the equitable amount of value capture by Value Creators.

The other key aspect of this story is Spotify's strategy of partnering with, investing in, or completely buying up Value Complementors, taking them from their Outer Value Network, into either their Inner Value Network (e.g., Tencent), or completely absorbing them into their business (e.g., Genius).

TURNING THE TABLES

Tidewave – turning the tables

This journey to scale is one which any entrepreneurial start-up will find itself on as it moves beyond proving its value proposition to working out how to scale the solution. Take the case of Tidewave, a successful Norwegian start-up which is now well advanced on the slopes of their version of climbing the Innovation Mountain, where we can see the same pattern of finding, forming and getting an ecosystem to perform.

Bedsores are bad news. Lying in bed all day might sound fun on a lazy Sunday morning with the newspapers and TV to entertain you, but spending days on end unable to move because of some debilitating illness or a broken bone is something different. The skin, especially in older people, rubs and scratches and pretty soon you have a pressure ulcer, a wound. Bedsores are sadly very common and, untreated, can lead to complications, especially if they become infected.

The best way to prevent bedsores is to keep moving – but with ill and incapacitated people, that's not always so simple. Nor is the alternative of having someone else help turn them; human bodies are surprisingly heavy and difficult to manoeuvre. So for nurses and carers there's a big physical challenge and a heavy workload to add to an already crowded working shift.

It's a significant issue in healthcare. Estimates suggest that one in five patients at European health institutions suffer from pressure ulcers and, apart from the painful patient experience, it is a high-cost problem. According to the Agency for Healthcare Research and Quality, these run at around $10 billion per year in the USA alone. So, there's plenty of incentive for innovators to work on finding solutions.

One person who joined the quest was Audun Haugs, a successful engineer and inventor. He figured that if it was difficult to move the patient then an alternative

TIP
You can find out more on the Tidewave story in a series of videos interviewing the founding team – the link is here:

solution lay in moving the bed, or more specifically, the mattress. He set about developing a mattress which could be used to keep the patient gently moving – lateral rotation therapy; not such a simple task since the movement needs to be specific enough to keep the patient from getting pressure sores but gentle enough not to wake them.

TURNING THE INNOVATION TIDE CAN TAKE A LONG TIME.

His idea for a curved turning mattress showed promise in terms of health improvements and this gave him the confidence to apply for and secure a patent. But his sudden death in 2008 meant that the project got put on hold.

Ten years later it came back to life. Haugs's granddaughter, Elen Haugs Langvik, was studying for a business degree at the University of Stavanger and as part of her course on entrepreneurship she had to undertake a project. Looking round for an idea for which she had to develop a business plan, she remembered his invention and decided to use that. Working alongside her colleagues Bjørn Lorentzen and Nina Fagerheim Åmodt, they developed and pitched their plan, not only scoring high marks but also planting the seed which led to the formation of their company, Tidewave.

That business has continued to grow successfully and now operates in several European markets. A brief timeline gives us an idea of the way in which they grew through building and managing an ecosystem.

VI CHAP — SCALE STORIES

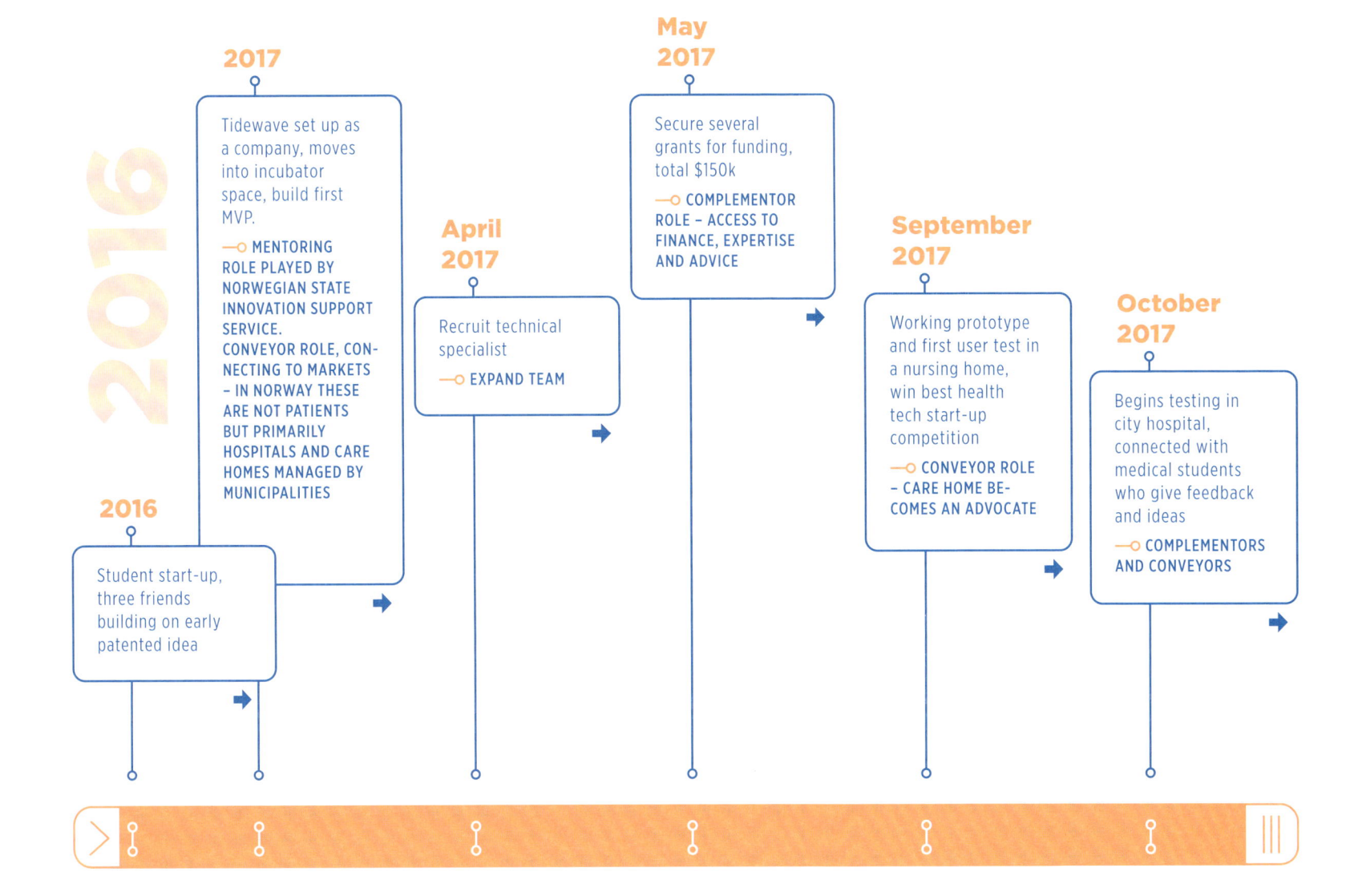

2016

Student start-up, three friends building on early patented idea

2017

Tidewave set up as a company, moves into incubator space, build first MVP.

—o **MENTORING ROLE PLAYED BY NORWEGIAN STATE INNOVATION SUPPORT SERVICE. CONVEYOR ROLE, CONNECTING TO MARKETS – IN NORWAY THESE ARE NOT PATIENTS BUT PRIMARILY HOSPITALS AND CARE HOMES MANAGED BY MUNICIPALITIES**

April 2017

Recruit technical specialist

—o **EXPAND TEAM**

May 2017

Secure several grants for funding, total $150k

—o **COMPLEMENTOR ROLE – ACCESS TO FINANCE, EXPERTISE AND ADVICE**

September 2017

Working prototype and first user test in a nursing home, win best health tech start-up competition

—o **CONVEYOR ROLE – CARE HOME BECOMES AN ADVOCATE**

October 2017

Begins testing in city hospital, connected with medical students who give feedback and ideas

—o **COMPLEMENTORS AND CONVEYORS**

PART 1   PREPARING FOR THE SCALING EXPEDITION

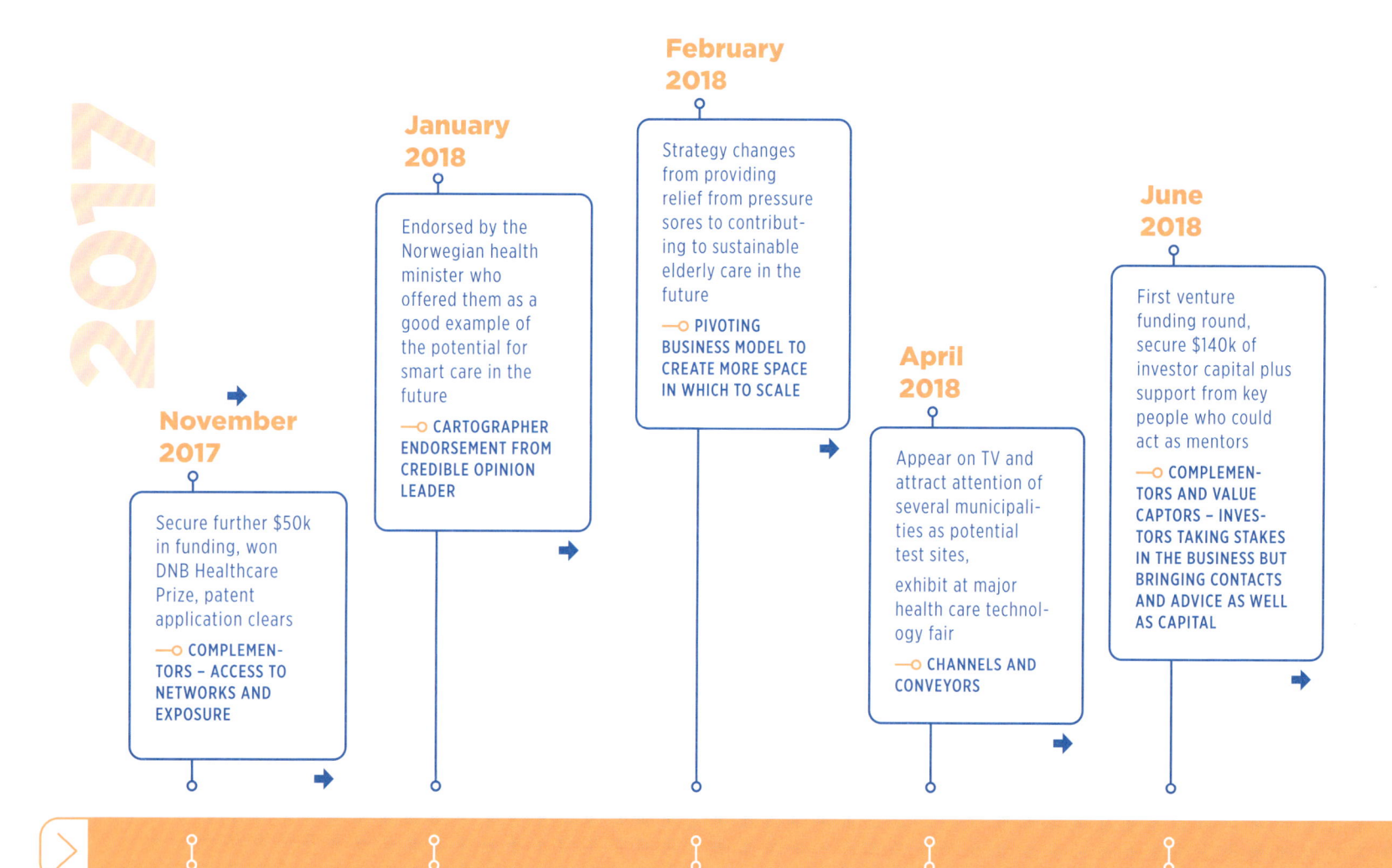

2017

November 2017
Secure further $50k in funding, won DNB Healthcare Prize, patent application clears
— COMPLEMENTORS – ACCESS TO NETWORKS AND EXPOSURE

January 2018
Endorsed by the Norwegian health minister who offered them as a good example of the potential for smart care in the future
— CARTOGRAPHER ENDORSEMENT FROM CREDIBLE OPINION LEADER

February 2018
Strategy changes from providing relief from pressure sores to contributing to sustainable elderly care in the future
— PIVOTING BUSINESS MODEL TO CREATE MORE SPACE IN WHICH TO SCALE

April 2018
Appear on TV and attract attention of several municipalities as potential test sites,

exhibit at major health care technology fair
— CHANNELS AND CONVEYORS

June 2018
First venture funding round, secure $140k of investor capital plus support from key people who could act as mentors
— COMPLEMENTORS AND VALUE CAPTORS – INVESTORS TAKING STAKES IN THE BUSINESS BUT BRINGING CONTACTS AND ADVICE AS WELL AS CAPITAL

CHAP VI — SCALE STORIES

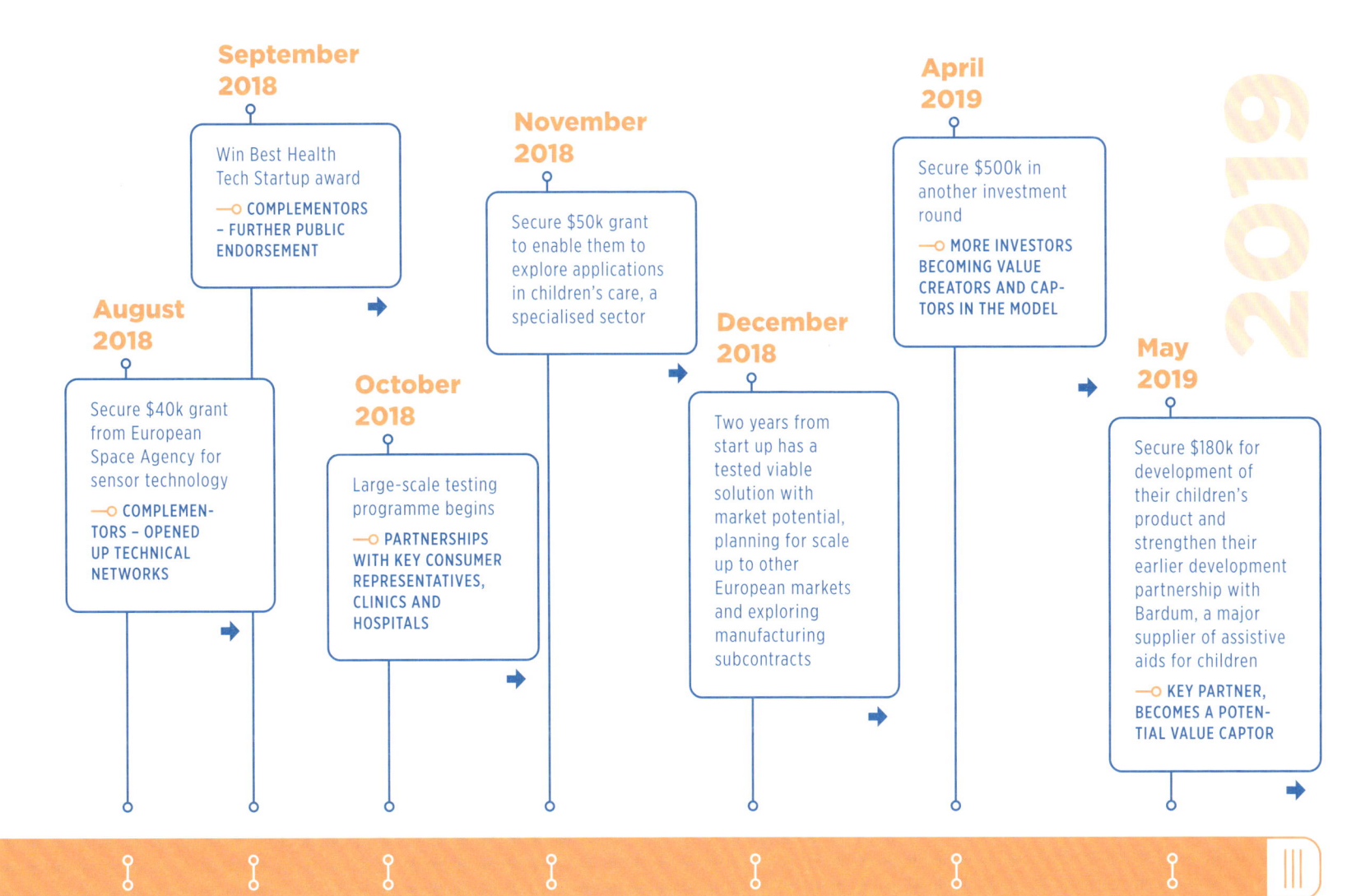

August 2018
Secure $40k grant from European Space Agency for sensor technology
—○ COMPLEMENTORS – OPENED UP TECHNICAL NETWORKS

September 2018
Win Best Health Tech Startup award
—○ COMPLEMENTORS – FURTHER PUBLIC ENDORSEMENT

October 2018
Large-scale testing programme begins
—○ PARTNERSHIPS WITH KEY CONSUMER REPRESENTATIVES, CLINICS AND HOSPITALS

November 2018
Secure $50k grant to enable them to explore applications in children's care, a specialised sector

December 2018
Two years from start up has a tested viable solution with market potential, planning for scale up to other European markets and exploring manufacturing subcontracts

April 2019
Secure $500k in another investment round
—○ MORE INVESTORS BECOMING VALUE CREATORS AND CAPTORS IN THE MODEL

May 2019
Secure $180k for development of their children's product and strengthen their earlier development partnership with Bardum, a major supplier of assistive aids for children
—○ KEY PARTNER, BECOMES A POTENTIAL VALUE CAPTOR

PART 1   PREPARING FOR THE SCALING EXPEDITION

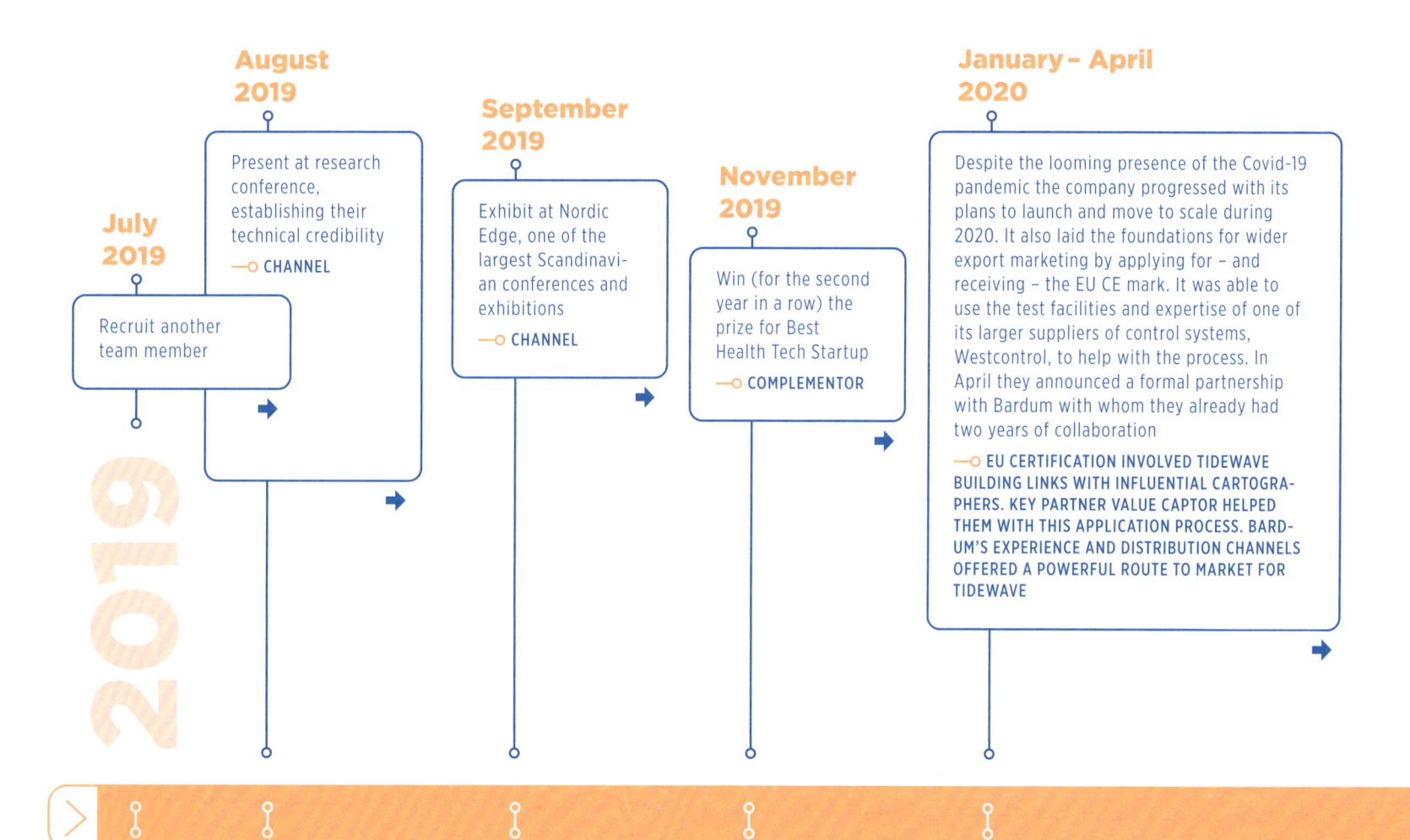

July 2019
Recruit another team member

August 2019
Present at research conference, establishing their technical credibility
— CHANNEL

September 2019
Exhibit at Nordic Edge, one of the largest Scandinavian conferences and exhibitions
— CHANNEL

November 2019
Win (for the second year in a row) the prize for Best Health Tech Startup
— COMPLEMENTOR

January – April 2020
Despite the looming presence of the Covid-19 pandemic the company progressed with its plans to launch and move to scale during 2020. It also laid the foundations for wider export marketing by applying for – and receiving – the EU CE mark. It was able to use the test facilities and expertise of one of its larger suppliers of control systems, Westcontrol, to help with the process. In April they announced a formal partnership with Bardum with whom they already had two years of collaboration

— EU CERTIFICATION INVOLVED TIDEWAVE BUILDING LINKS WITH INFLUENTIAL CARTOGRAPHERS. KEY PARTNER VALUE CAPTOR HELPED THEM WITH THIS APPLICATION PROCESS. BARDUM'S EXPERIENCE AND DISTRIBUTION CHANNELS OFFERED A POWERFUL ROUTE TO MARKET FOR TIDEWAVE

2019

VI SCALE STORIES

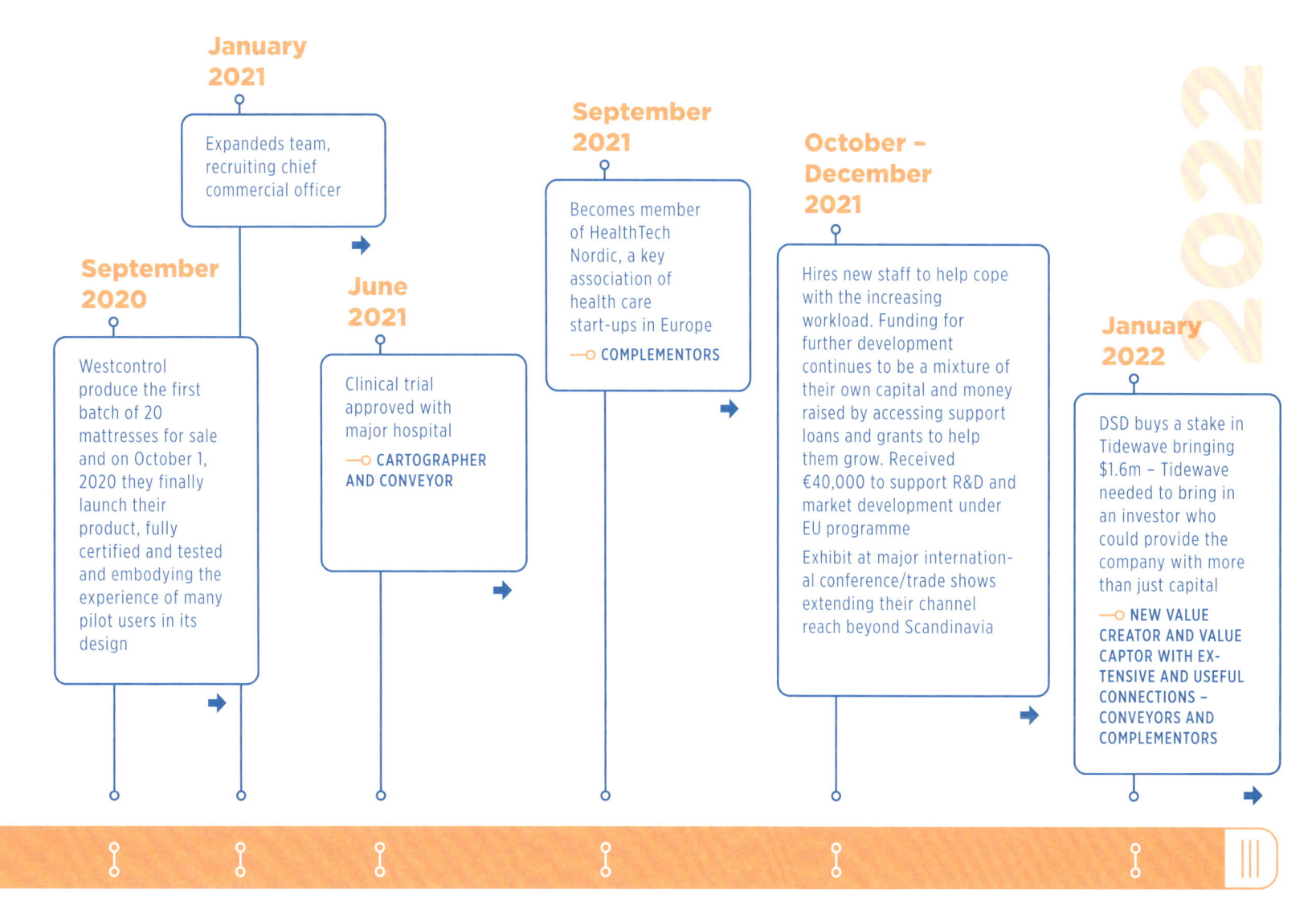

2022

September 2020

Westcontrol produce the first batch of 20 mattresses for sale and on October 1, 2020 they finally launch their product, fully certified and tested and embodying the experience of many pilot users in its design

January 2021

Expandeds team, recruiting chief commercial officer

June 2021

Clinical trial approved with major hospital

—○ **CARTOGRAPHER AND CONVEYOR**

September 2021

Becomes member of HealthTech Nordic, a key association of health care start-ups in Europe

—○ **COMPLEMENTORS**

October – December 2021

Hires new staff to help cope with the increasing workload. Funding for further development continues to be a mixture of their own capital and money raised by accessing support loans and grants to help them grow. Received €40,000 to support R&D and market development under EU programme

Exhibit at major international conference/trade shows extending their channel reach beyond Scandinavia

January 2022

DSD buys a stake in Tidewave bringing $1.6m – Tidewave needed to bring in an investor who could provide the company with more than just capital

—○ **NEW VALUE CREATOR AND VALUE CAPTOR WITH EXTENSIVE AND USEFUL CONNECTIONS – CONVEYORS AND COMPLEMENTORS**

NETFLIX

Tidewave are still in the middle of their journey to scale. But what does it look like from further up the mountain slope? What's the picture as we look back from somewhere near the top, when our innovation has scaled and we are having a significant impact on our chosen market? Let's climb in a helicopter for a moment and fly up to that particular viewpoint; let's look at the case of Netflix.

The home entertainment market is huge and estimates suggest that streaming services account for a big part of it. There are some big players involved – Disney, Sony, Amazon and, particularly, Netflix. In 2022 Netflix reported subscriber numbers of 223 million (and this doesn't include the number of households who share passwords (and hence access) to their services. They are continuing to grow; that figure (from Q3 2022) represented an advance of 2.5 million on the previous quarter despite increasing competition and the sudden surge in the cost of living putting a squeeze on disposable income.

Impressive scale – and yet that wasn't quite the picture when it all began. Once upon a time (so the story goes) Netflix co-founder Reed Hastings was annoyed at having to pay penalty fees for returning films late to his local Blockbuster store. He saw a value proposition in an alternative model based on mail order and without late fees, etc.

It was based on a rental/subscription model; he told some friends about it and they sketched out what it might look like and what they would need to make it work. Their original model was a very simple Value Network linking consumers (people who want to watch movies) with a supply side (moving a stock of films via some kind of order processing and then sending them to the right customer using a delivery service). Films could then be returned by the customer without late fees and the process could start again.

They moved to pilot the idea, learning about the wrinkles and challenges to help adapt it and make it robust. Their approach began with a manageable local area and was gradually extended and replicated. Part of that learning was about channels and conveyors. The team realised that there were additional players on the

TIP
There's a useful blog and video exploring Netflix's history at this link:

CHAP VI — SCALE STORIES

NETFLIX'S JOURNEY TO SCALE WAS NOT A SIMPLE STROLL ALONG A WELL-MARKED PATH; IT INVOLVED A LONG-TERM EXPEDITION INTO UNCERTAIN TERRITORY.

channel side, like delivery company DHL, and that it might help to have multiple carriers. All the time the team were trying to balance their financial model; they had to borrow money to get things started and investors want a return, becoming Value Captors who have to be managed. They also expanded the value creation side by upgrading their sales order processing capability by commissioning a bespoke system instead of using an Excel spreadsheet.

They also faced growing competition; others saw the potential in the idea (including Blockbuster who explored a similar model). And they were aware of a growing trend towards people watching online channels directly rather than using DVD players.

In other words, they began life in classic start-up territory, gradually moving beyond pilots towards the foothills of the Innovation Mountain. Let's try and map the rest of their journey on a timeline.

TIP
You can find another analysis of Netflix using a variety of business strategy tools here:

PART 1   PREPARING FOR THE SCALING EXPEDITION

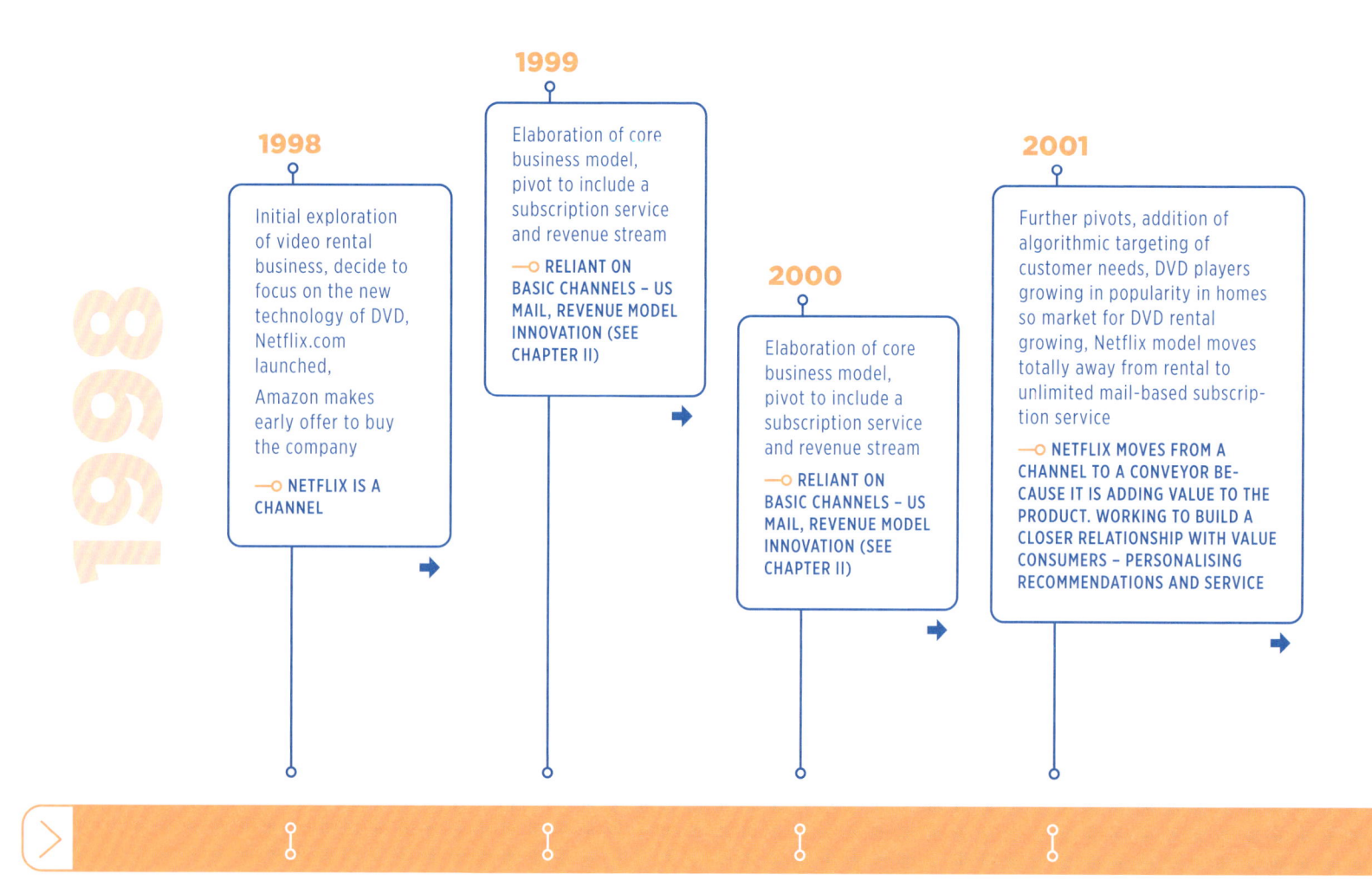

1998
Initial exploration of video rental business, decide to focus on the new technology of DVD, Netflix.com launched,

Amazon makes early offer to buy the company

—o **NETFLIX IS A CHANNEL**

1999
Elaboration of core business model, pivot to include a subscription service and revenue stream

—o **RELIANT ON BASIC CHANNELS – US MAIL, REVENUE MODEL INNOVATION (SEE CHAPTER II)**

2000
Elaboration of core business model, pivot to include a subscription service and revenue stream

—o **RELIANT ON BASIC CHANNELS – US MAIL, REVENUE MODEL INNOVATION (SEE CHAPTER II)**

2001
Further pivots, addition of algorithmic targeting of customer needs, DVD players growing in popularity in homes so market for DVD rental growing, Netflix model moves totally away from rental to unlimited mail-based subscription service

—o **NETFLIX MOVES FROM A CHANNEL TO A CONVEYOR BECAUSE IT IS ADDING VALUE TO THE PRODUCT. WORKING TO BUILD A CLOSER RELATIONSHIP WITH VALUE CONSUMERS – PERSONALISING RECOMMENDATIONS AND SERVICE**

CHAP VI — SCALE STORIES

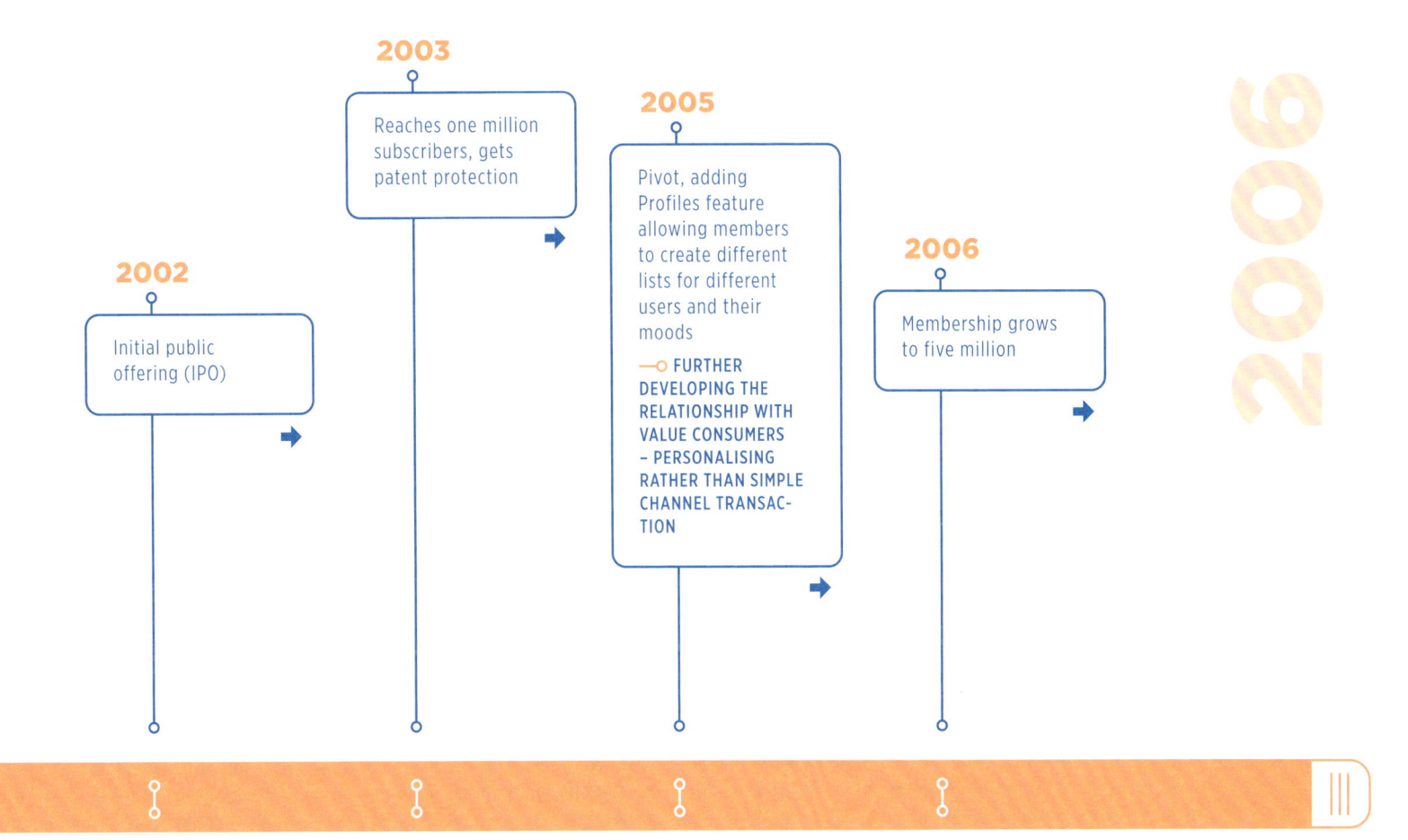

2002
Initial public offering (IPO)

2003
Reaches one million subscribers, gets patent protection

2005
Pivot, adding Profiles feature allowing members to create different lists for different users and their moods
— **FURTHER DEVELOPING THE RELATIONSHIP WITH VALUE CONSUMERS – PERSONALISING RATHER THAN SIMPLE CHANNEL TRANSACTION**

2006
Membership grows to five million

2006

PART 1   PREPARING FOR THE SCALING EXPEDITION

2007

Move to streaming model replacing the mail-based channels and system, runs in parallel for a while since they only had 1,000 films available for streaming, compared to 70,000 available on DVD

—o **SHIFT IN VALUE CHANNELS, ABILITY TO REACH MORE PEOPLE AND MUCH FASTER, NO GEOGRAPHICAL BOUNDARIES (POTENTIALLY RADICAL CONVEYOR SHIFT)**

2008

Netflix partners with consumer electronics brands to allow streaming on Xbox 360, Blu-ray players and TV set-top boxes

In August 2008, the Netflix database is corrupted and the company was not able to ship DVDs to customers for three days, leading the company to move all its data to the Amazon Web Services cloud

—o **ADDS VALUE COMPLEMENTORS AS PARTNERS BUT ALSO GAINS ACCESS TO NEW CONSUMERS AND NEEDS PARTNERS (AWS) TO HELP DELIVER STREAMING EXPERIENCE (COMPLEMENTOR/CHANNEL)**

2009

Netflix streams overtake DVD shipments, the $1 million Netflix Prize is awarded to a team able to improve accuracy of recommendations by 10 %, streaming partnerships expand to internet-connected TVs as membership surpasses 10 million, Netflix's culture deck is published

—o **FURTHER REFINING THE RELATIONSHIP MODEL BINDING VALUE CONSUMERS CLOSELY THROUGH IMPROVED PERSONALISATION, CULTURE DECK IS EXAMPLE OF CODIFYING MINIMUM VIABLE BUREAUCRACY**

2010

Moves into new geographical territory – arrives in Canada, spreads platform to include mobile phones, targets kids as a key new segment

In August 2010, Netflix reaches a five-year deal worth nearly $1 billion to stream films from Paramount, Lionsgate and Metro-Goldwyn-Mayer. It also acquires the rights from Sony for a series called Breaking Bad which the original broadcaster (AMC) were going to cancel after its 3 seasons. The launch on Netflix of the previous episodes boosts the viewing figures for AMC's 4th series and doubles them by the time a 5th series is launched. This complementary viewing pattern has been termed the Netflix effect.

—o **EXPANDS VALUE CONSUMER BASE, EXTENDS CHANNELS TO INCLUDE MOBILE MARKET, EXTENDS PERSONALISATION MODEL TO KIDS SECTOR, INCREASING PARTNERSHIPS WITH CREATORS AND DEALS WITH CONTENT PROVIDERS, ACKNOWLEDGED AS A CONVEYOR BY THE STUDIOS, NOT JUST CONSUMERS**

CHAP VI — SCALE STORIES

2011

Further geographical scaling, Netflix launches in Latin America and the Caribbean, the first Netflix button appears on remote controls

Netflix's streaming business becomes the largest source of internet streaming traffic in North America, accounting for 30% of traffic during peak hours

Netflix announces a content deal with DreamWorks Animation

— **MOVING IN THIS DIRECTION MEANS COLLABORATING WITH TV REMOTE CONTROL MANUFACTURERS BUT IN DOING SO OPENS UP A NEW CHANNEL WITH WHICH TO ENGAGE VIEWERS AS END USERS**

2012

Membership reaches 25 million members and expands into the United Kingdom, Ireland and the Nordic countries, begins commissioning its own content

Netflix and Disney announce an exclusive multi-year agreement for first-run United States subscription television rights to Walt Disney Studios' animated and live-action films

Netflix files with the Federal Election Commission to form a political action committee called FLIXPAC. Netflix spokesperson Joris Evers states that the intent is to engage on issues like net neutrality, bandwidth caps, usage-based billing and the Video Privacy Protection Act

— **NETFLIX BECOMES A DIFFERENT KIND OF VALUE CREATOR: WHERE BEFORE IT WAS PLAYING A VALUE-ADDED CHANNEL/CONVEYOR ROLE, IT NOW MOVES INTO CONTENT CREATION DIRECTLY, OPENS UP NEW CHALLENGES AROUND VALUE COMPETITORS, IT INVOLVES EXPANSION INTO PARTNERSHIPS WITH NEW PLAYERS ON DELIVERY, WRITING, RIGHTS, ETC. AND NEW COMPETITORS AND BUMPING INTO REGULATION ETC., BEGINS TO CREATE THE PLATFORM ROLE FOR ITSELF, WORKING WITH CARTOGRAPHERS**

2013

Creative content creation becomes a major part of the model with shows like *House of Cards, Hemlock Grove, Arrested Development* and *Orange Is the New Black, House of Cards* goes on to win three Primetime Emmy awards – the first for an internet streaming service

The Profiles and My List features debut on streaming

PART 1   PREPARING FOR THE SCALING EXPEDITION

2014

Membership surpasses 50 million and extends to Austria, Belgium, France, Germany, Luxembourg and Switzerland, begins streaming in 4K Ultra HD

Netflix discovers that Comcast Cable was slowing its traffic down and agrees to pay to directly connect to the Comcast network

—○ **ISSUES WITH VALUE CHANNEL, NEEDS A FORMAL AGREEMENT TO DEAL WITH THIS, BRINGING COMCAST IN FROM THE OUTER VALUE NETWORK INTO NETFLIX'S INNER VALUE NETWORK**

2015

Launches first original feature film, *Beasts of No Nation,* first non-English original series, *Club de Cuervos,* and first Asian original, *Terrace House* debuts. Membership extends to Australia, Cuba, Italy, Japan, Spain and New Zealand

Audio descriptions for the visually impaired launches with *Daredevil*

Scaling across language and cultures, becoming truly global

—○ **INVOLVES NEW AND DIFFERENT VALUE CONSUMERS**

2016

Expands to 130 new countries, bringing the service to members in more than 190 countries and 21 languages around the world, the Download feature is added for offline and on-the-go viewing

VI SCALE STORIES

2017

Membership hits 100 million members globally, wins its first Academy Award for *The White Helmets*, impact is now not only commercial and reach but also cultural, winning Oscars

The introduction of interactive storytelling and the Skip Intro button gives members more choices to tailor their viewing experience

Signs a music publishing deal with BMG Rights Management, iterates a goal of having half of its library consist of original content by 2019

—○ EXTENDING CONTENT DEAL INTO MUSIC TO HELP SUPPORT NETFLIX-CREATED CONTENT

2018

Becomes the most nominated studio at the Emmys, winning 23 for series including *GLOW, Godless* and *Queer Eye*. PIN protection is rolled out as part of several parental control enhancements

2019

Wins four Academy Awards for *Roma* and *Period. End of Sentence* and debuts its first original animated film with *Klaus*. New production hubs open in London, Madrid, New York and Toronto. *Black Mirror: Bandersnatch* wins the first major Emmy for an interactive title. The ecosystem is now a cultural impact as much as a service delivery, attracts writers and pitches, becomes a key employer of actors, etc.

Covid-19 forces people to spend much more time at home, boosts consumption and interest

Increasing competition and loss of access to content, Disney ended the agreement set up in 2012

—○ VALUE CREATOR BECOMES VALUE COMPETITOR

2020

Top 10 lists debut, allowing members to see what's popular for the first time. Netflix is the most nominated studio at the Academy Awards and Emmys

Hardship Fund launches to aid creative community workers impacted by Covid-19, recognising the ecosystem's dependence on actors and writers/creators

2021

Increasing competition from other players like Disney+, Apple and Amazon ratchet up access problems around content and subscribers, forces Netflix to rely even more on its own (costly) content-creation model

Explores possible entry into games market, hiring experts and publishing plans to add video games by 2022, trial offerings launched in Poland

Netflix Originals made up 40% of Netflix's overall library in the United States

Continuing investment in physical production facilities, signs a long-term lease deal with Aviva Investors to operate and expand the Longcross Studios in Surrey, UK

Expanding into books and storytelling/sharing, announces the launch of the Netflix Book Club where readers will hear about new books, films and series adaptations and have exclusive access to each book's adaptation process. Netflix will partner with Starbucks to bring the book club to life via a social series called *But Have You Read the Book?*

In compliance with the EU Audiovisual Media Services Directive and its implementation in France, Netflix reaches commitments with French broadcasting authorities and film guilds, as required by law, to invest a specific amount of its annual revenue into original French films and series. These films must be theatrically released and would not be allowed to be carried on Netflix until 15 months after their release

—o **JUST AS NETFLIX HAS MOVED FROM CONVEYING TO CREATION OF ORIGINAL CONTENT, NOW ORIGINAL CONTENT PROVIDERS WERE MOVING INTO BECOME COMPETITTORS IN THE THE CONVEYING MARKET. ISSUES WITH CARTOGRAPHERS IN THE FRENCH MARKET**

2022

Is the second largest entertainment/media company by market capitalisation as of February 2022

As of September 2022, Netflix has 222 million subscribers worldwide, including 73.3 million in the United States and Canada, 73 million in Europe, the Middle East and Africa, 39.6 million in Latin America and 34.8 million in the Asia-Pacific region, it is available worldwide aside from Mainland China, Syria, North Korea and Russia

Netflix plays a prominent role in independent film distribution and is a member of the Motion Picture Association

CHAP VI SCALE STORIES

ICE-CREAM DREAMS

Carlo Gatti

The challenge of scaling innovation isn't a new one as this case highlights. Carlo Gatti was born in the Italian part of Switzerland and moved to England in 1847 where he earned a living running a stall in Holborn, London, selling waffles, chestnuts and other delicacies. By 1849 he'd managed to open a small restaurant where he specialised in chocolate and ice cream, something which delighted customers since it was the first shop to offer what had previously been a treat for the wealthy who could afford their own icehouse.

His reputation spread and Gatti realised that in order to expand to meet this demand he was going to need a lot more of the key resource in ice-cream making – ice. He set up a contract with the Regent's Canal Company who had developed techniques for harvesting the frozen water from the canal during the winter months and preserving it in an icehouse to be available for sale throughout the year.

He expanded his channels, opening another stall in 1851 near Charing Cross station to tap into the commuter traffic, and he pioneered the idea of selling a → 'PENNY LICK' – a portion of ice cream in a glass dish sold for one penny. And, not surprisingly, others began to enter the market, offering their version of ice cream to a rapidly expanding market amongst the population of Victorian London. And it didn't take long before the idea spread to other cities.

Gatti was a shrewd businessman and expanded his ice business, selling to these entrepreneurs. He built a huge ice warehouse capable of storing tons of ice in a deep ice well in 1857. By 1862 he'd sunk a second deep well and was having to extend his supply lines, importing ice all the way from Norway and transferring it by barge from

→ **PENNY LICK**
The 'penny lick' is an early example of a 'Base of the Pyramid' strategy.

CONVEYOR ROLE
Gatti moved into a conveyor role for ice, from his creator role as an ice cream seller.

the docks of the River Thames using the canal network. Pretty soon he was the biggest ice importer in London.

He rode a wave of public interest in refrigeration; increasingly people began to use domestic iceboxes and larders to preserve food and he was able to meet their needs by operating a fleet of delivery carts selling door-to-door. He was able to use the profits to expand his restaurant business and open new branches; in later years he diversified into the music hall business where he was able to offer ice cream as part of the interval refreshments. He died in 1878 having earned the reputation as the 🔗 *Ice-Cream King* of Victorian England.

From an innovation scaling point of view we can see a familiar pattern. Gatti began as a value creator and pioneered a product, acting as an enthusiastic conveyor, exhibiting and selling wherever he could reach people. He was fortunate to have some complementors, in particular a cookery writer, Agnes Marshall, whose 1888 cookbook included a recipe for 'cornets with cream', which was perhaps the first published version of what became the ubiquitous ice-cream cone. It did her reputation no harm; she became known as the 'Queen of Ices'. She helped position ice cream as a standard dish

🔗 **TIMELINE HISTORY OF ICE CREAM**

FROM CAKES AND CANALS TO BEING CROWNED THE 'ICE-CREAM KING' OF ENGLAND – A SUCCESSFUL JOURNEY TO SCALE.

on the menu of households who could increasingly afford to buy ice from a local icehouse and store it in their own ice box.

So, the successful scaling of ice cream as an innovation wasn't a lucky accident or the inevitable outcome of having a good value proposition. It depended on finding, forming and getting a Value Network to perform as an effective ecosystem

MANY ROADS TO ROME

Let's look now at how scaling can take different paths, even in otherwise crowded markets. This next case looks at how building a community can help – essentially focusing on making the complementors part of the IVN.

Giffgaff is a UK subsidiary of the giant Telefonica operation launched in 2009 and has successfully carved out a niche in the highly competitive mobile phone marketplace. It is a mobile virtual network operator and is the third largest in the UK after Tesco Mobile and Virgin Mobile; it makes use of the O2 network in the UK and EU, operated by Telefonica.

The basic model is a network run without call centres and high-street shops and is built around members, not customers, who would get rewarded for active participation.

It has close to four million users and continues to grow. Its core differentiator is that it has built a community of users who actively co-create and market the service and in doing so become not only Value Consumers but also Value Creators. It's where the name → 'GIFFGAFF' comes from; it is originally a Scottish phrase meaning 'mutual giving'. As a result its net promoter score (a measure of customer satisfaction and loyalty) is way above the industry average, helping protect its competitiveness.

Giffgaff manages to keep costs down by making use of this online user community rather than a customer support team. While that may not seem ideal, it came out top in a recent Ofcom report into mobile customer satisfaction. Its on-site FAQ and community message boards are excellent and provide answers to even the most niche of questions.

→ **GIFFGAFF**
Giffgaff shows how an entity (in this case the user community) can play different value roles at the same time.

GIFFGAFF VALUE NETWORK

NETWORK ROLE	VALUE CREATOR(S)	VALUE CAPTORS	VALUE CONVEYORS	VALUE CHANNELS
KEY PLAYERS	Giffgaff and its community	Giffgaff and its parent, Telefonica	O2 network in the UK (owned by Telefonica)	Social media
NATURE OF RELATIONSHIP	Co-creation across community	Formal ownership	Formal service-level agreements but supplemented by virtue of being community led rather than supported by a call centre or high-street shop	

SCALE STORIES

VALUE COORDINATORS	VALUE COMPETITORS	VALUE CARTOGRAPHERS	VALUE COMPLEMENTORS	VALUE CONSUMERS
Giffgaff community	Other mobile operators	Ofcom – the national regulatory body	The giffgaff community	The giffgaff community – close to 4 million users
Strong participation reinforced by rewards and by peer-to-peer loyalty	Giffgaff differentiates itself in a crowded market by its emphasis on co-creating community	Lobbying via Telefonica parent	Strong and innovative, many useful new service ideas emerging from the ongoing ideal labs	Strong through building a sense of shared ownership and co-creation

CONNECTING THE WORLD

🔗 *Canals have had a big influence on innovation* – you could say they helped to change the world. Way back in the days of the early industrial revolution in England it was clear that waterways could offer the means of transportation of the raw materials and fuels going into the factories and the finished goods coming out of the 'workshop of the world' for global distribution. The trouble was that simply digging a hole and filling it with water wasn't going to get you very far – what you needed was systems thinking.

This is what James Brindley had in abundance as he pioneered his canal engineering revolution and took the potential of the innovation to scale. Water was at the centre of his thinking; he seemed to have an intuitive grasp of how it flowed and how those principles could be applied in a wide variety of situations.

And of course one thing about water is that it requires you to think in systems terms – how things are linked together. Brindley had a gift for seeing the interconnected challenges in realising big schemes like the mine pumping system – and for focusing on how to enable the whole system to deliver value. At a technical level he pioneered a wide range of technological innovations including lock systems, pumping machinery and cutting narrower canals which reduced water consumption.

But his genius extended beyond the technical sphere; he was also skilled at ecosystem building. Whether it was working with cartographers – spending a great deal of time lobbying to get local and sometimes national government approval for his plans – or partnering with investors to recruit them as Value Creators and Captors, he knew the importance of systems thinking around value. He was a skilled Value Coordinator, creating a platform model which engaged Value Consumers from raw material suppliers, through to the factories which used his canals to ship their products. He literally created a channel (his canals) which others paid to use, and he was a vocal and effective conveyor of the idea of canals as an alternative to roads as the core of industrial transportation.

He was also something of a visionary, spotting innovation opportunities ahead of their time. His narrow boats were nicknamed 'starvationers' on account of

---

🔗
'GOING WITH THE FLOW'

Also available as podcast.

the wooden braces across the hull which gave them strength. They looked like an emaciated torso, but this design meant they were strong enough to haul tons of coal or iron ore. But there was a bottleneck in terms of loading and unloading and so Brindley designed a system of wooden containers for coal which could be filled and transhipped easily. His first boat with 10 containers began work in 1766; it proved the concept but its widespread implementation was left to a man called James Outram who linked the idea into a system in which horses pulled containers from mines along rails to the canal where they were quickly transhipped. As the railways emerged to replace horse-drawn traffic, this ➜ INTERMODAL SYSTEM took off.

As we saw earlier this model had considerable potential – the revolution which Malcolm McLean brought about some 200 years later with the containerisation of global shipping. The extent to which we've come to depend on containerisation is captured beautifully in the image of the container carrier Evergreen, which got stuck in the Suez Canal on March 23rd, 2021 for six days, creating a supply chain problem which took the rest of 2021 and beyond to resolve.

McLean's innovation did not scale easily and he had to work to build and manage his Value Network. One of his first moves was to try and acquire the Pan-Atlantic Steamship Company which had docking rights at key port cities. But he hit a major cartographic problem when the railroad companies attempted to block the deal on anti-trust grounds.

This forced his hand and he sold his trucking company and gambled on buying the shipping line, renaming it Sea-Land Industries. He bought two old tankers and retrofitted them to carry his containers. The SS Ideal X embarked on its maiden voyage in April 1956, carrying 58 containers from New Jersey to Houston.

Having proved the concept, he became an activist channel, working hard to convince key consumers of the potential of his system. It helped that he could offer them lower transportation costs, safer storage and cheaper insurance; at the same time he wooed another Value Consumer group – the port authorities – by demonstrating his system would enable them to reduce port costs and still remain profitable. But he also had to work hard at another cartographic problem; the big labour unions were active in trying to block his system because of its serious implications for their members.

➜ **INTERMODAL SYSTEM**
A transportation system which combines different modes of transportation, for example railways and canals, or road and sea.

By the late-1960s, Sea-Land Industries was the largest shipping company in the world with more than 27,000 containers, 36 ships covering 30 major ports. The underlying economics were transformational. In 1965 a ship could expect to remain in port being loaded or unloaded for up to a week, with transfer rates for cargo around 1.7 tonnes per hour. By 1970 this had speeded up to 30 tonnes per hour and big ships could enter and leave ports on the same day. Journey times from door-to-door were cut by over half and the ability to seal containers massively cut losses due to theft and consequently reduced insurance costs.

NOT JUST COMMERCIAL MARKETS

Can't Wait to Learn (CWTL) is a set of offline self-paced educational game applications accessed on tablet computers that take children through a government-approved curriculum, providing them an opportunity to work toward primary-level education. In this way, CWTL reinforces the education pipeline across informal and formal education, to decrease dropout rates and encourage transitions into formal primary education. The secret ingredient? CWTL's unique co-creation process with children culminates in the development of locally contextualised game content, including the design, characters, storyline and curriculum.

CWTL offers a local interface that reflects children's reality, which lowers the threshold for children to engage, particularly if new to technology. Characters developed through the co-creation process guide children through the games, which allow them to learn at their own pace. Children discover how their skills are applicable in their own lives – and how they can improve the lives of people surrounding them.

CWTL started in 2012 as an idea and prototype in Sudan. Since then it has scaled across five countries. At the start of the journey a group of partners came together (UNESCO, Al Afad University, War Child) to start developing curricula and test various protocols/modalities. War Child then took on the challenge of hosting the project and trialling the first product, which turned into a lead role in testing and scaling the innovation. This meant partners were in place from the start to develop the curriculum and gamification and to help with trialling the games with children. As the innovation continued to develop, and research was carried out on its impact,

CAN'T WAIT TO LEARN

the internal team in War Child Holland needed to grow. The first recruits all came into this small but energetic team.

A key stage in the development was the realisation that the number of partnerships required for funding, product development and implementation meant that the innovation leader needed to adapt their role. Plotting the scale journey, managing the operations and engaging with all the partners and stakeholders was no longer possible. The importance of the growing Value Network needed to take priority, so an operations manager position was brought in to the team to release the director to manage this Value Network.

During the prototyping and piloting phase, decision criteria for partners had been linked to the value needs at that time, but this changed over time, with the CWTL team bringing in some of the value creation roles in house by moving away from a partner to develop the curriculum, taking on that role themselves.

Another key learning was regarding conveyors, with the software company they had partnered with being unable to scale at the same speed that they needed to expand across new countries. This necessitated a need to change conveyors when it came to software development and technical support.

The CWTL story is one of needing to reconfigure the roles both it and its partners played through the scaling journey. We will return to CWTL later on.

Liverpool Football Club

Ian is a Liverpool FC fan. Over the past decade or so he's watched the development of a group of complementors appear around the club that are an excellent example of how you can increase value, and also potentially destroy it as an innovator.

The story starts in October 2010, when Liverpool Football Club (LFC), one of the world's most recognisable football brands, was close to being declared bankrupt. In stepped John W. Henry and Fenway Sports Group (FSG) to purchase the club. Henry and his co-investors knew that LFC was an undervalued asset that had the potential to be restored to one of the most successful clubs in Europe, and to be scaled into the growing markets of Asia and America.

THE VALUE OF LFC
In October 2010, as Liverpool Football Club was on the brink of insolvency, investors sensed that LFC was an undervalued asset that had the potential to once again become one of the most successful clubs in Europe.

A key theme in the story is the way in which the fans played both a role in ousting one group of owners, leading to the sale of the club and then became key complementors for the new owners of LFC. The way the previous LFC owners had run the club had led to growing fan activism to try and oust them from the club. This took the form of a football supporters' union called Spirit of Shankly in 2008 and the development of other fan groups, such as Spion Kop 1906. It also saw a reinvigoration of fan culture, with groups using the emergence of social media to organise and give them a strong identity.

FSG the new owners quickly saw the potential in leveraging the fan base to help them grow the club; they began exploring ways of leveraging LFCs fans and their culture as a unique selling point and differentiator. They would use the fan culture as a complementor.

Football fans of different football clubs have their own unique cultures. In the case of Liverpool it revolved around three things – Liverpool Football Club, music and fashion. Supporters groups like Spion Kop 1906 and Spirit of Shankly became a focus for mobilising this culture, but this period of protest also saw the emergence of fashion brands, music artists and events and an explosion of social media enterprises.

THE FANS' UNIQUE CULTURE
Recognising the untapped potential of the fan base, FSG, the new owners, swiftly embraced the idea of harnessing Liverpool FC's supporters to facilitate the club's growth. They actively sought opportunities to leverage the fans' unique culture as a distinctive selling point and differentiator, considering the fan culture as a valuable complement to their endeavors.

THE PERIOD OF PROTEST SAW THE EMERGENCE OF FASHION BRANDS, MUSIC ARTISTS AND EVENTS, AND AN EXPANSION OF SOCIAL MEDIA BUSINESSES AROUND LIVERPOOL FOOTBALL CLUB.

VI SCALE STORIES

Examples of the way this culture worked to create a strong identity – that LFC could leverage as part of their brand:

- *Fashion – quite apart from the official insignia and replica jerseys fans established their own designs, local shops and online stores. The explosion in internet shopping meant that aspiring fans from all over the world could now be part of fan culture by buying the latest T-shirt online.*

- *Supporting LFC – Liverpool fans were at the forefront of a new wave of fan media that emerged from friendships forged in the heat of battle against the previous owners. To supplement the fanzines that already existed came podcasts and YouTube channels. Some of these grew to significant influence; for example the Anfield Wrap podcast quickly grew from a group of fans putting out a weekly podcast to an influential media group putting out three to five shows a day. A YouTube channel ('The Redmen TV') went from around 5,000 subscribers after their first season to over half a million subscribers today.*

- *Music – What started as a few friends gathering to sing Liverpool songs after the match in a city centre pub became the launch pad for two UK top 10 albums for their star performer, Jamie Webster. The nights moved from pubs, to warehouses, to concert halls on to stadiums. They formed the basis for huge concerts; for example on the Champions League final days in which LFC competed they attracted crowds of up to 60,000 people.*

This ecosystem of Liverpool fans doing what they loved best, and creating successful commercial ventures from it, helped spread the Liverpool fan brand around the world. The fan-culture brand is inextricably linked to the club, but it is completely independent from it. A symbiotic relationship which, to quote Neil Atkinson from the Anfield Wrap, means that "when Liverpool wins, we all win."

LFC have in the main leveraged this vibrant fan culture to great success. But their recent history highlights the importance of managing relationships with complementors and the risks if that relationship is compromised. In 2016 LFC sought to increase revenue from

FAN CULTURE BRAND

Liverpool fans' entrepreneurial spirit and love for the club have created a successful fan culture brand that has gained worldwide recognition, independent from the club itself.

THE SPIRIT OF SHANKLY SUPPORTERS

Liverpool FC suffered a blow to their brand image and points chase because they disregarded warnings from the Spirit of Shankly supporters' union, who acted as cartographers.

ticket sales. For them it seemed a rational decision; partly due to its origins as a club located in a working class area of a working class city, ticket prices were lower than comparable clubs like those based in London. Accordingly they announced that they would be changing prices for a number of tickets for the coming 2016/17 season. Their highest 'normal' seat would now cost £77.

Before setting the price, LFC had consulted with supporters groups but did not confirm with them the prices they finally set. The response by these two groups was one of anger; they felt that the pricing was exorbitant and called for direct action by fans – requesting that they leave the next home game on the 77th minute (effectively 15 minutes early) to register their opposition to the price hike.

When the day came, LFC were cruising to a 2-0 home win, when on the 77th minute around 10,000 fans got up from their seats and left. The team collapsed and let in two late goals to draw the game 2-2. The images of fans streaming out chanting against the price hike was shown across the world. LFC had shot their brand image, and their points chase, in the foot by not heeding warnings from a cartographer in the form of the Spirit of Shankly supporters' union.

What followed was a public apology from the club and a reduction in the top ticket price. It also subsequently inspired mass protests across the country by fans of other clubs. This eventually led to the Premier League club owners agreeing to capping away tickets at £30 – another blow to the revenue stream that LFC were trying to increase.

This crisis highlights not only the power of fans as complementors but also the way in which this power can effectively turn complementors into cartographers, rewriting the rules by which LFC could operate. In this case LFC learned from their mistakes and brought representatives of the fans into their Inner Value Network through the creation of a Supporters Board.

But relationships across Value Networks need constant review and adaptation. In 2019 LFC's fortunes were riding high, thanks to both the team's performance on the pitch and the strong support from the growing supporter base. Scenes such as the post-Champions League win parade which saw 750,000 fans line the streets of Liverpool to welcome the winning team home were beamed across the world.

In trying to leverage the commercial revenue, from this strong position, LFC focused on several strategic areas including challenging the growth of counterfeit merchandise. They tried to trademark the name Liverpool in eight different classes associated with football merchandise. But one of those classes, Class 35, was a direct threat to the ecosystem of shops and traders that had exploded around LFC as part of the fan ecosystem. These fashion brands were not copying LFC merchandise, but rather creating their own designs with imagery and phrases of Liverpool and their players. Their T-shirts and sweatshirts were not only sported by fans, but also worn prominently by famous ex-players on TV and online.

Fan activism kicked in again and Liverpool fans bombarded the airwaves, the club and lawyers protesting the move. LFC tried to counter this by explaining that they weren't trying to run the local businesses into the ground, but rather were targeting industrial-level counterfeiting in the Asian market that was eroding their value capture. But the strength of the fan base showed through again in its potential to become a cartographer: the UK's Intellectual Property Office threw the application out. Once again LFC had to come out and apologise to their fan base and work to reset their relationship with this key part of their Value Network. «

CHAPTER VI — SUMMARY
WHAT YOU HAVE LEARNED IN THIS CHAPTER

▷ This chapter has presented a variety of different case studies of innovators at various points in their scaling journeys.

▷ It highlights the many ways in which the journey plays out but in particular the importance of configuring and then managing a Value Network.

PART 2

WORKING ON YOUR JOURNEY TO SCALE

CHAPTER VII
BASE CAMP VISIONING:
WHERE ARE WE GOING? _____ 142

CHAPTER VIII
SOLUTION _____ 154

CHAPTER IX
ORGANISATION _____ 174

CHAPTER X
BOOKENDS _____ 184

CHAPTER XI
MOVERS _____ 196

CHAPTER XII
SHAPERS _____ 206

CHAPTER XIII
DEVELOPING VALUE NETWORKS _____ 214

CHAPTER XIV
SCALE STRATEGY _____ 228

CHAP VII
BASE CAMP VISIONING: WHERE ARE WE GOING?

In order to start our scale journey we need to set up base camp and identify the 'team' (Value Network) we have to pull together. We need to identify the peak we are trying to scale. To sketch out the potential route, and then identify where our next camp will be once we cross the initial chasm.

Both John and Ian live near the top of hills in the same county in the UK. One looks over a valley with a river flowing into the English Channel in the south of the county, while the other lives on a hill overlooking the North Atlantic in the north of the county. These two beautiful panoramas have helped us with the challenge of writing this book.

So, we suggest you inspire yourself for the scaling expedition you are about to embark on by envisioning what the panorama will look like when you reach scale. In order to cross the chasm, and to battle through the messy and miserable middles, you need to have a scale panorama to cling to. And that's what this chapter is all about.

In order to go to scale, we need to have a good view of how high the summit we are trying to reach is. What does scale mean for us? How long will it take us to reach?

WHAT DOES SCALE MEAN FOR US? HOW LONG WILL IT TAKE US TO REACH?

We see scale as realising the maximum potential value of an innovation or new enterprise. This can be on a number of spectra, whether it is measured in number of users, number of consumers, value of the company, global expansion, level of social impact, etc. Each innovation and enterprise will have its own view on what type of scale they are aiming at. What is certain though is that scaling takes a long time!

CREATING A SCALE PANORAMA

If we are going to be in for a long haul it's worth having a clear idea of where we're aiming to get to, a star we can steer our journey by. This is why we advise innovators to have an end game in mind: what will the view from the top of the scaled summit look like? We call this the scale panorama – what we can see from the top of the mountain, looking down and looking back at the path we have taken. In order to build the scale panorama, we're going to need:

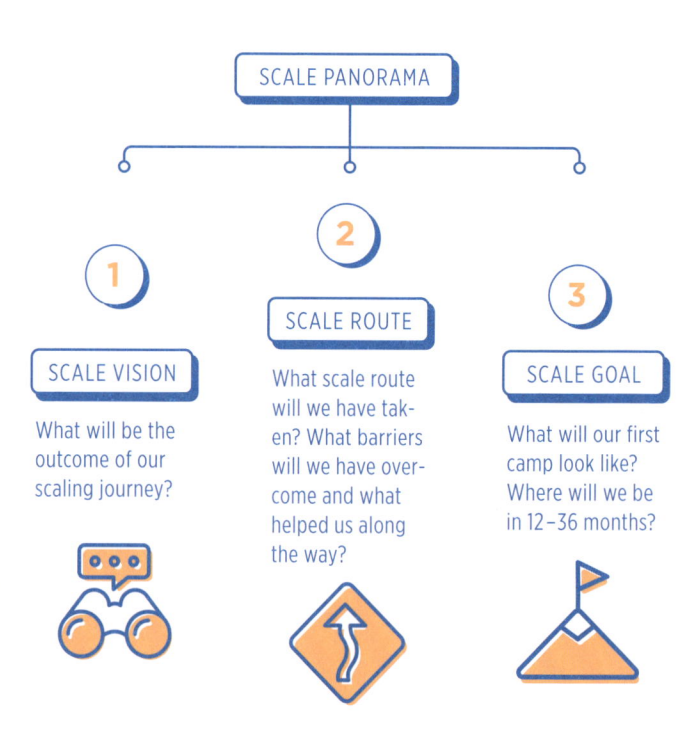

TIP
You can find these tools on our website:
www.scalingvalue.org

SCALE PANORAMA

1 SCALE VISION
What will be the outcome of our scaling journey?

2 SCALE ROUTE
What scale route will we have taken? What barriers will we have overcome and what helped us along the way?

3 SCALE GOAL
What will our first camp look like? Where will we be in 12–36 months?

BASE CAMP VISIONING: WHERE ARE WE GOING?

Scale vision

As we have seen, there are no overnight success stories, so set a long-term vision of what scale looks like. This should be a short statement that will look different from sector to sector, but will usually outline the following:

▷ <u>Timeframe</u>: When will you reach your vision? We recommend 10+ years
▷ <u>Value created</u>: What value is being delivered?
▷ <u>Consumer reach, market share or impact</u>: Be tangible with the numbers – no one is going to hold you to them specifically, but it creates a shared understanding in the team, across the organisation and with key stakeholders, like investors, of the size of your scale ambition.
▷ <u>Geographical reach</u>: Where is your market? Is it in one country, in a region or global?

EXAMPLE › WHAT'S YOUR SCALE VISION?
Try to complete the sentence below for your innovation …

EXAMPLE

In a decade _EducAItion Ultd_ will be _delivering personalised teaching_ for _100 million primary school children_ in _the South Asia and Sub-Saharan Africa markets_.

MY SCALE VISION

In a decade _____ will be
name of innovation

_____ for
type of value creation

_____ in
number and type of Value Consumers

_____ .
number of countries/regions

Scale route

If you are going to reach the scale peak, what route will you take? Every mountain has multiple routes that can be taken. Some are well-worn paths, while others are scaling rock faces that no one has yet attempted. Which one is the right one for you?

This will be dictated by a number of different factors: ease of the route, speed with which you can scale, experience in that type of journey, industry norms. Although your particular ascent will be unique to your organisation, there are some routes that are well worn. We outline some of the most common routes here.

TIP
You can try out a number of routes to scale, you don't have to choose just one.

COMMON ROUTES TO SCALE
Different typologies

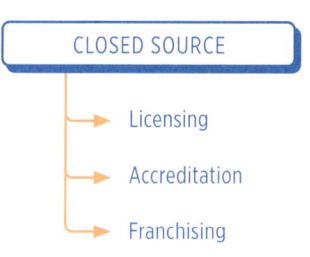

- OPEN SOURCE
  - + Community
  - + Training
  - + Consultancy

- CLOSED SOURCE
  - Licensing
  - Accreditation
  - Franchising

VII BASE CAMP VISIONING: WHERE ARE WE GOING?

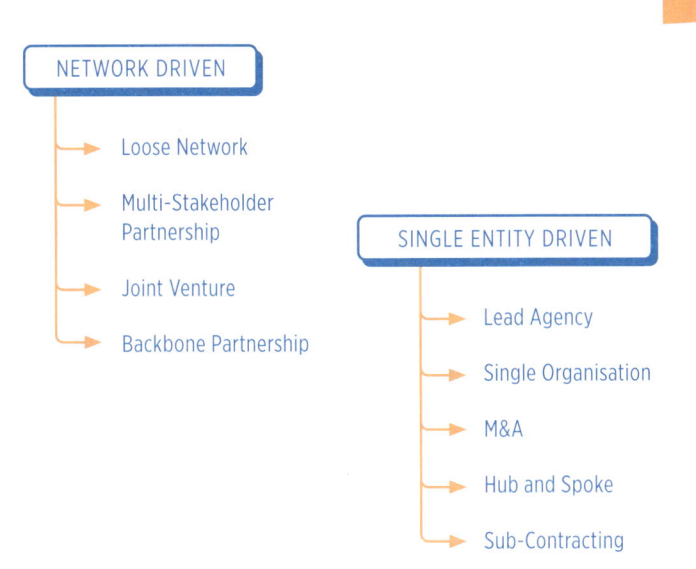

TWO FACTORS ARE CRITICAL TO THINK ABOUT – HOW MUCH CONTROL WILL YOU HAVE AND HOW MANY PARTNERS WILL YOU BE WORKING WITH?

NETWORK DRIVEN
- Loose Network
- Multi-Stakeholder Partnership
- Joint Venture
- Backbone Partnership

SINGLE ENTITY DRIVEN
- Lead Agency
- Single Organisation
- M&A
- Hub and Spoke
- Sub-Contracting

However, there are two factors that we believe are the most important: How much control you will have using a particular scaling route; and how numerous your inner Value Network partners will be on the route.

These two factors have a significant impact on your scaling journey. They are particularly important for both the type of organisation you will need to develop and how you configure your innovation.

PART 2   WORKING ON YOUR JOURNEY TO SCALE

CONTROL – COMPLEXITY SPECTRUM

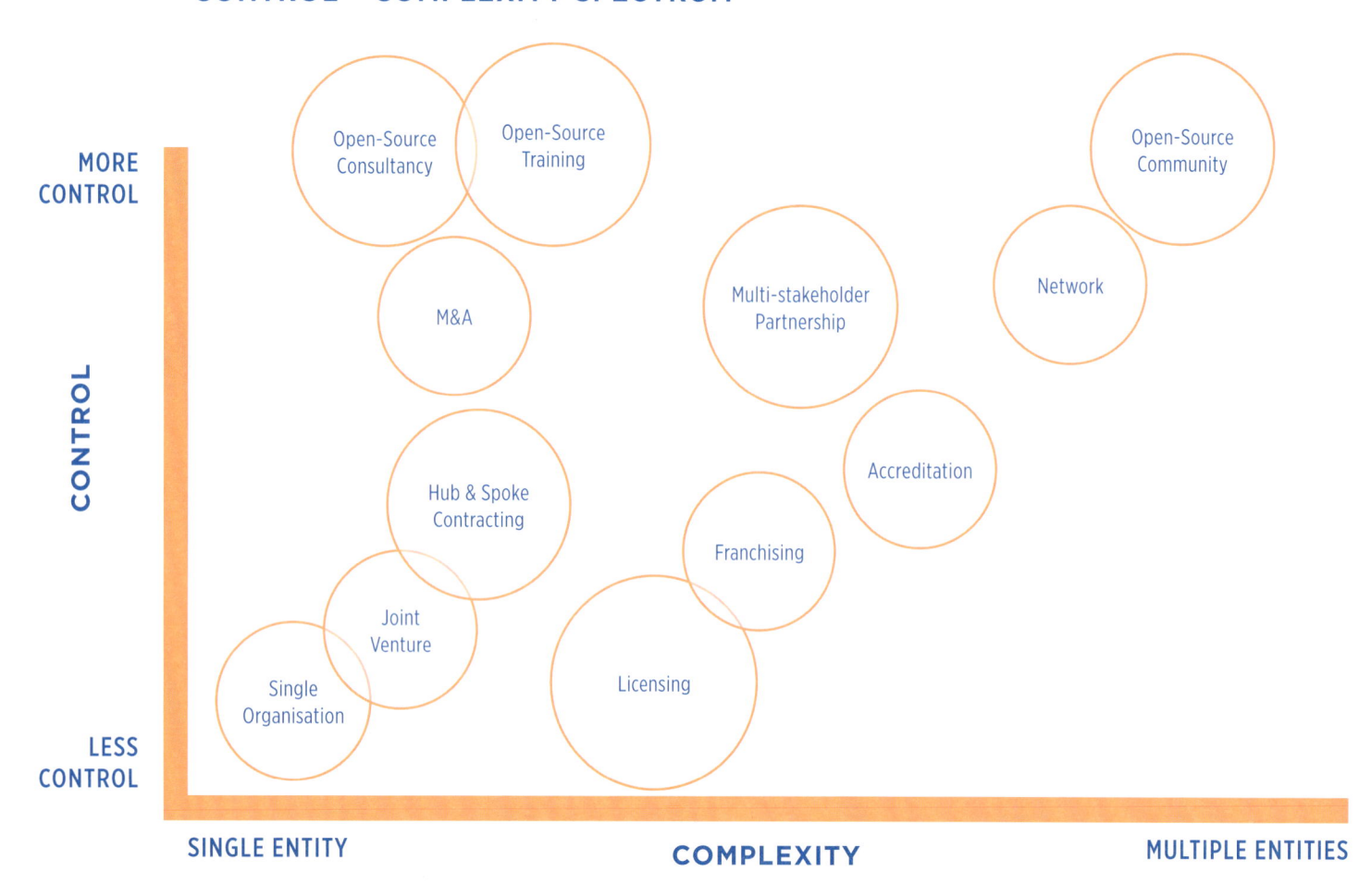

CONTROL (MORE CONTROL ↑ / LESS CONTROL ↓)

COMPLEXITY (SINGLE ENTITY → MULTIPLE ENTITIES)

- Open-Source Consultancy
- Open-Source Training
- Open-Source Community
- M&A
- Multi-stakeholder Partnership
- Network
- Hub & Spoke Contracting
- Accreditation
- Franchising
- Joint Venture
- Single Organisation
- Licensing

VII BASE CAMP VISIONING: WHERE ARE WE GOING?

EXAMPLE › IDENTIFY YOUR ROUTE

How will you have gotten to scale? Underneath your scale vision, write down your route and the obstacles you will have overcome and the critical success factors. We will have reached our scale vision through [Ministries of Education] *route/s*.

BARRIERS

BARRIER 1
Teachers' resistance to change

BARRIER 2
Government's regulation of AI

BARRIER 3
Large Language Model availability for non-major languages of instruction

CRITICAL SUCCESS FACTORS

CSF 1
Our intellectual property

CSF 2
Endorsement of the World Federation of Teachers Unions

CSF 3
Expansion of low cost internet connectivity through low orbit satellites

TIP
You can try out a number of routes to scale, you don't have to choose just one.

The scale routes we show above are not the only ones, but they are some of the most common. You may want to explore another route, or may want to create a hybrid or try out a few routes. The key is to be able to visualise the route/s and ensure that it is in the right area of the control-complexity spectrum. This will provide you with a basis to make decisions on your innovation and organisation as you move forward.

Each route up the mountain will involve surmounting obstacles and will require some critical success factors. Anticipate them and visualise them. You can't know all of the obstacles ahead of time, nor can you anticipate what all the ingredients for success will be (although we will provide you with many in this book). However, you can anticipate some. They might be obstacles of investment or technology difficulties, or of competition or regulations. Your critical success factors could be retaining your start-up culture as you grow or key partnerships you make. Envisioning them enables you to fill in the missing middle and prepare for the messy and miserable middles you will face.

YOU CAN'T ANTICIPATE EVERYTHING – BUT YOU CAN MAKE SURE YOU TRY TO IMAGINE ALL THE POSSIBLE CHALLENGES YOU FACE – BEFORE YOU BUMP INTO THEM!

Scale goal

Agreeing on the peak you are trying to scale and the route you want to take is critical – the vision will be your north star and the route will be your best guess at the way you will scale. However, you need to also establish where your first camp after base camp will be on your ascent. We call this your scale goal. It is identifying where you want to get to on the next stage of your scale journey.

This goal is constructed in a similar fashion to the scale vision, the main difference being that the timeframe will be shorter. We recommend a minimum of 12 months and a maximum of three years. This provides you with enough time to make significant steps forward, but is not too far ahead that the goal is likely to be out of date or have completely changed before you are even halfway there.

It is important to note that the scale route for reaching your scale goal may not be the route you choose for your 10-year scale vision. In our experience this is often the case. For example, sometimes innovation teams or start-ups will choose to use a few strategic partners to test out how implementable their processes are by another organisation before moving to a franchising model. Other internal start-ups might see the next 12 months within the parent company before spinning out to achieve their scale vision.

EXAMPLE › SCALE GOAL

Within the next 12-36 months, EducAltion Ultd will have piloted personalised maths education modules for 50,000 primary school children in Bangladesh and Namibia through partnerships with local education charities.

SCALE PANORAMA

Now that you have completed these tasks, you are in the position of having a completed scale panorama.

PART 2   WORKING ON YOUR JOURNEY TO SCALE

EXERCISE › SCALE PANORAMA

SCALE VISION

In a decade _____[name of innovation]_____ will be _____[type of value creation]_____ for _____[number and type of value consumers]_____ in _____[number of countries/regions]_____.

We will have reached this by overcoming these barriers:

- **BARRIER OVERCOME 1**
- **BARRIER OVERCOME 2**
- **BARRIER OVERCOME 3**

And our critical success factors to achieving scale will have been:

- **CSF 1**
- **CSF 2**
- **CSF 3**

SCALE GOAL

Within the next 12–36 months _____[name of innovation]_____ will have _____[type of value creation]_____ for _____[number and type of value consumers]_____ in _____[number of countries/regions]_____ through _____[route]_____.

You can use this panorama as a device for inspiring the team and helping them visualise success. It is also a tool for quickly explaining your proposed scale strategy to other key stakeholders, such as investors and partners.

The next step is to see how well equipped you are for this ascent. We will look at your innovation, your organisation and your Value Network to see if they are up for the challenge.

Before you embark on the journey from base camp, we want to provide you a health warning. We talked in Chapter II about the three middles of scaling – missing, messy and miserable. Are you prepared for these middles?

CHAPTER VII — SUMMARY
WHAT YOU HAVE LEARNED IN THIS CHAPTER

Scaling takes time, often more than a decade. So, you need patience and you need determination. In this chapter you have:

▷ Created your scale vision.

▷ Identified your proposed scale route and spotted the barriers you will overcome and the critical success factors that have got you to the top of the mountain.

▷ Identified where your first camp on the expedition will be (your scale goal).

▷ Put together a scale panorama to share your aspirations within your team and beyond.

CHAP VIII

SOLUTION

> This chapter provides tools and guidance on the proof, replicability and defensibility of your innovation, product, service or process. At the end of the chapter there will be a checklist for you to assess where you have gaps.

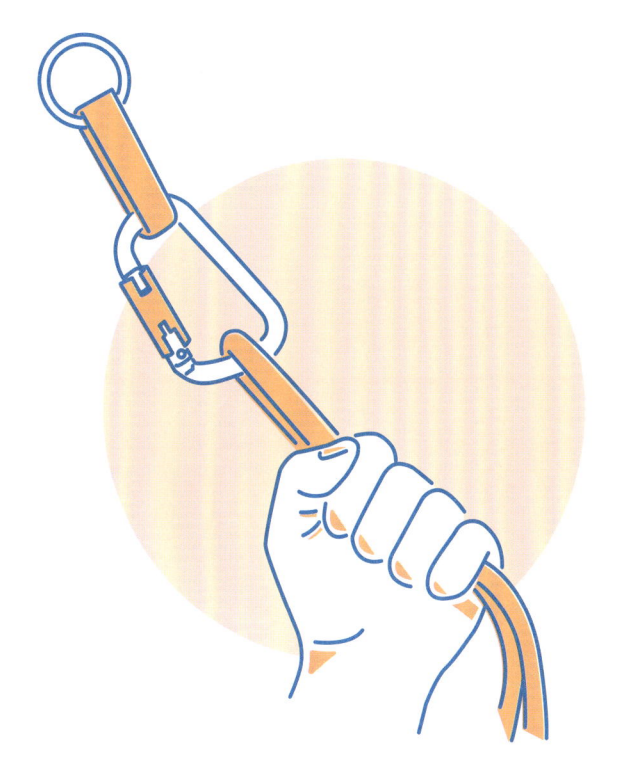

STRESS TEST YOUR INNOVATION TO MAKE SURE IT IS SCALABLE

IS OUR SOLUTION SCALABLE?

At the heart of → AGILE INNOVATION, which has become widely used as a way of managing innovation projects, is the idea of taking a lean, entrepreneurial, iterative approach. And central to this approach is the idea of testing and experimenting to gain consumer feedback. This is done by creating varying degrees of minimum viable product (MVP) or service (MVS) to test with those consumers.

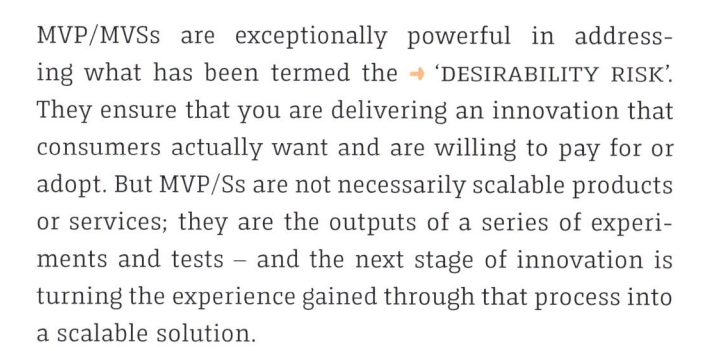

MVP/MVSs are exceptionally powerful in addressing what has been termed the → 'DESIRABILITY RISK'. They ensure that you are delivering an innovation that consumers actually want and are willing to pay for or adopt. But MVP/Ss are not necessarily scalable products or services; they are the outputs of a series of experiments and tests – and the next stage of innovation is turning the experience gained through that process into a scalable solution.

In order to make a solution truly scalable, a number of things need to be completed. Firstly, you need to address longer-term questions of desirability, i.e., start providing confidence to the Value Consumer that this is

→ **AGILE INNOVATION**
is an approach to managing innovation which allows for fast learning and pivoting.

→ **DESIRABILITY RISK**
is ensuring that your Value Consumers not only like your product or service, but that they are willing to adopt it, and in most cases, pay money for it.

Bland, D.J. & Osterwalder A. (2019). *Testing Business Ideas: A Field Guide for Rapid Experimentation*, Hoboken NJ: Wiley.

a product, service or process that they can rely on. What we call 'proven'.

Then there is the need to ensure that your innovation can effectively scale, and do so in a sustained manner. We call this 'replicable'. Thirdly, capturing value from your innovation as it scales, and ensuring that this value creation and capture isn't easily copied, is critical. This is what we call 'defendable'.

Proven

There are a number of ways to prove your innovation, but these three approaches are key:

- *A clear value proposition* – it has to be crystal clear to the Value Consumer what the purpose of the innovation is and what value it creates for them

- *It needs to be adoptable* – the innovation needs to be as easy to adopt and use as is possible

- *It needs to have evidence of value* – the innovation needs to have proof that it delivers the value it promises

A clear value proposition

When developing your MVP, and even when piloting your innovation in the real world, you must foster a close link to the consumers in order to create an innovation that meets their needs. You often have time to build a rapport – if not a relationship – with them and can therefore have quality time to explain how your innovation will deliver value for them.

This isn't possible when going to scale. You need a clear and concise value proposition; one that can work for multiple audiences across multiple geographies, cultures and languages. The value proposition should be clear and consistent. It's useful to have multiple versions ranging from a simple one-sentence description through to a full-page specification, each bringing in more detail.

TIP

Checking out and updating your solution is a key first step in scaling – you can find some tools to help with this on our website: www.scalingvalue.org

CHAP VIII — SOLUTION

DUCKDUCKGO: SHORT AND SWEET

The web browser DuckDuckGo gets straight to the point with a question that, if you answer yes to, will lead you more than halfway towards using their product:

In five very short sentences they have clearly articulated their value proposition. They haven't even bothered to tell you their function, i.e., a search engine. They just tell you what their value is.

Refining your value proposition statements by interacting with your target Value Consumers is critical. Communicating your value proposition is central to scaling, so it's worth bringing in external support if you don't have a marketing capability.

> **Tired of being tracked online? We can help.**

> **We don't store your personal info. We don't follow you around with ads. We don't track you. Ever.**

EXERCISE › WRITE YOUR VALUE PROPOSITION IN MULTIPLE FORMATS

In business-to-consumer (B2C) markets you often only get a few seconds to get your value proposition across. In this case, what is it?

In business-to-business (B2B) markets, you sometimes have a bit more time to grab your customer's attention. In this case, what is your value proposition in a couple of paragraphs?

1

VALUE PROPOSITION

1–3 SENTENCES

2

VALUE PROPOSITION

1–2 PARAGRAPHS

VIII SOLUTION

In business-to-government (B2G) markets, you are often writing bid documentation, so how would you unpack your value proposition in a cover page or exec summary?

3
VALUE PROPOSITION

1 PAGE

Once you have completed this, you should ensure that it works, not just in your current market but also in the markets you are seeking to scale to. This is particularly the case for your strap lines; you don't want to fall into the trap Pepsi did with its launch into China with their slogan "Pepsi Brings You Back to Life" being translated to "Pepsi Brings Your Ancestors Back From the Dead".*

* www.snopes.com/fact-check/come-alive

Adoptable

We met Everett Rogers earlier – he was a pioneering map-maker for understanding the journey to scale and the chasm that has to be crossed. He identified five factors that influence adoption:

- Relative advantage: Is your innovation better than its competition?
- Compatibility: Does your innovation interact with the other elements around it seamlessly?
- Complexity: How hard is it to understand and use your innovation?
- Trialability: Can the buyer try before they buy?
- Observability: How easy is it to see the innovation and it's value in a crowded market place?

In his research, Rogers found that for innovations that had diffused (scaled) quickly, these five attributes explained over 50% of this high performance.

We therefore recommend stress testing your innovation for its adoptability to increase the speed at which your innovation will scale. We have adapted Rogers' factors to develop the Accelerating Adoption Tool for you to use to test your innovation.

VIII SOLUTION

161

EXERCISE › ACCELERATING ADOPTION TOOL

Is your innovation ready for adoption? Try using the 'Accelerating Adoption Tool' to explore this theme.

- RELATIVE ADVANTAGE
- OBSERVABILITY
- SIMPLICITY
- TRIALABILITY
- COMPATIBILITY

EVIDENCE OF VALUE

As we saw in Chapter II, the adoption process follows an S-curve and it's influenced by many factors. In particular, people are influenced by different kinds of evidence, so we need to be sure we're presenting our evidence in the best light and that it is targeted at the key decision-makers.

The trick is to understand what evidence is required for which stakeholder as different stakeholders will require different evidence. For instance, in pharmaceuticals, the regulator requires very different evidence to end consumers.

In order to address this, it's worth thinking about which stakeholders you need to provide evidence to, what the evidence is that they need, for what purpose, and finally, how and where you will present this to them. Not only will different stakeholders in your Value Network require different levels of robustness in the evidence, but they also will need convincing at either a head level or a heart level, and often a mix of both. Head-level evidence is things like facts and figures, whilst heart-level evidence is compelling stories and images. Understanding which of your stakeholders is convinced by which type of evidence will help you tell the story of what type of evidence they need, and how you should present it.

TIP
The Nesta Standards of Evidence paper provides a useful guide on how to think about evidencing your innovation.

EVIDENCE MATTERS IN SCALING INNOVATION – WITHOUT IT, IT'S GOING TO BE HARD TO CONVINCE ADOPTERS, INVESTORS AND PARTNERS TO COME ON BOARD.

CHAP VIII SOLUTION

EXERCISE › EVIDENTIARY REQUIREMENTS

This tool helps you assess what types of evidence are needed for your key value role stakeholders and what the strength of evidence you currently have is. It also prompts you to identify where you might need to develop more evidence to bring them on board with your innovation.

HEAD EVIDENCE

ROBUSTNESS OF OUR EVIDENCE

EVIDENCE TO HAND

_____
_____
_____

ROBUSTNESS OF EVIDENCE REQUIRED

ADDITIONAL EVIDENCE REQUIRED

_____
_____
_____

VALUE ROLE: _____

HEART EVIDENCE

CURRENT EVIDENCE ENGAGEMENT LEVEL

EVIDENCE TO HAND

_____
_____
_____

REQUIRED EVIDENCE ENGAGEMENT LEVEL

ADDITIONAL EVIDENCE REQUIRED

_____
_____
_____

EXERCISE › EVIDENTIARY REQUIREMENTS

← IN THIS EXERCISE, YOU CAN CARRY OUT THE FOLLOWING STEPS

1 Identify which value role you are analysing (you will need to complete one of these for each value role persona you require evidence for)

2 Start with 'Head Evidence'. How robust is your evidence? (1 brain = e.g., anecdotal evidence, 5 = e.g., multiple randomised control trials)

3 What is that evidence? (Describe it out under 'Evidence at Hand')

4 Using the same brain scale as Step 2, how robust does your evidence need to be?

5 What evidence will you need to gather (e.g., through research, user testing) to reach this level of robustness?

6 Move on to 'Heart Evidence'. How much does your evidence and the way you present it engage the stakeholder's heart?

7 What level of engagement are you going to need?

8 What evidence will you need to gather (e.g., case studies, images, stories) to reach this level of engagement?

REPLICABILITY

Replicability is at the heart of scaling. It is the thing that has driven the largest global transformations from products or services. Examples include:

- *Printing press*: *The ability to replicate texts quickly and accurately led to a revolution in mass literacy and the democratisation of knowledge*

- *The Twelve Steps*: *The codification of a 12-step process by the Alcoholics Anonymous organisation has led to the scaling of the process to over 180 countries*

- *McDonald's*: *The codification of recipes and processes enabled McDonald's to use franchising to expand to over 100 countries and ensure consistency in the process*

- *Aravind Eye Care System*: *The strict codification of a cost-effective cataract procedure and rigorous training allowed the expansion of the Aravind Eye Care System for cataract removal to scale. The same model has been used for many other common procedures such as perinatal maternity treatment (🔗 LifeSpring Hospitals) and heart bypass surgery (🔗 NHL Hospitals)*

Replicability is about making sure we are scaling under control – and the key to doing this effectively lies in three key steps:

- *Codification*: *The process of taking what is in someone's head, documenting and potentially automating it*

- *Core, modular and hackable*: *The process of deciding which parts of your innovation are the same everywhere (core), which you provide the user choice over (modular) and where the user can add their own modifications or additions (hackable)*

- *Lifecycle*: *The process of ensuring that your innovation delivers value for the consumer, wider society and the environment from design all the way through to end-of-life recycling or disposal*

CASE STUDY ON LIFESPRING HOSPITALS

CASE STUDY ON NHL HOSPITALS

Codification

Codification is the process of turning tacit knowledge into shared knowledge, written knowledge and ultimately automated knowledge. The level of codification used for each component of your innovation will be different, e.g., for an innovative way of delivering training you may codify the material in a physical training manual, whilst you might automate the participant registration on an online learning management system.

We can think of several levels of codification; the framework on the right of this page is a helpful checklist.

In our codification exercise you can assess how codified each of your innovation's components are now and the level of codification they will need to be able to scale. You can also assess whether they are core, modular and hackable. We then encourage you to think about how the codification will happen and when it should be completed by.

SERVICE MAPPING
Kimbell, L. (2015). *The Service Innovation Handbook.* Amsterdam: BIS.

LEVELS OF CODIFICATION

- 0 — Inside one person's head
- 1 — Inside several individuals' heads
- 2 — Can be shown
- 3 — Can be shown and described verbally
- 4 — Is written down or drawn in a document
- 5 — Can be systematically replicated based on documentation
- 6 — Is partially automated
- 7 — Is fully automated

CHAP VIII SOLUTION

CODIFICATION METHODS
Examples of ways in which knowledge can be codified.

1. PROCESS MAPPING

This is an exercise that should be carried out to codify any processes in your innovation. We recommend carrying it out with all the people involved in that process. It is also an excellent tool for not only mapping the process as it is, but also improving the process.

2. SERVICE MAPPING

This is similar to process mapping but is particularly focused on interaction points between your innovation and the Value Consumer. (→ p. 166)

3. SHADOWING AND OBSERVING

A good business analyst is worth their weight in gold! If you can have someone observe or shadow a process, procedure, training or design session, and have them document it, you will often be able to codify quite rapidly.

4. DOCUMENTING

Sometimes, you just need to get the most knowledgeable people on the innovation component to document the key aspects to it.

5. AUTOMATION

If your component is already written down, or even built and is working well, you may want to automate it. Automation is effectively taking the responsibility for an action away from the user, by either building it into the physical redesign of the product, or creating a mechanised or digitised action that takes the action/step out of the user's hands.

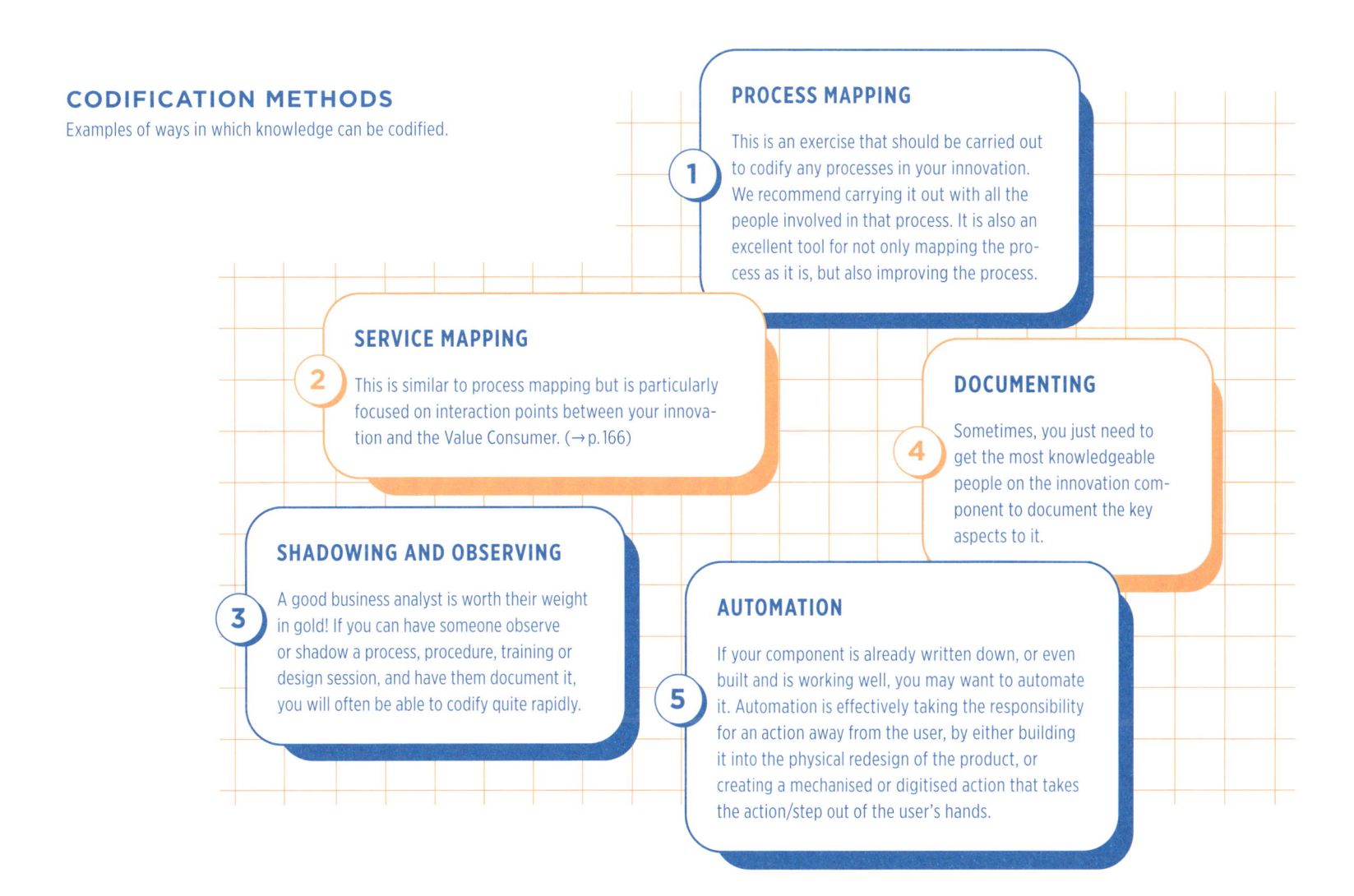

Core, modular and hackable

By the time you get to the scaling stage with your innovation it will be a combination of products, processes, services, procedures, policies and behaviours. It is complex! You have now distilled that complexity into component parts in the codification exercise.

Once you have identified the key components in your innovation, you then need to decide which components are:

- *Core: Exactly the same for everyone who interacts with the innovation*
- *Modular: The consumer has a choice over whether to use the component or not (you provide the options or permit linkages to external options, e.g., through → APIs)*
- *Hackable: The consumer can add their own things to the innovation that you are not providing or supporting*

The art of scaling is getting the balance right between the consistency and the customisability of your innovation. The more modular and hackable the solution is, the more contextual and personalised the consumer can make it, potentially driving adoption. However, it often means that it is also more expensive to develop and maintain, and there is a higher likelihood of reducing adoption due to complexity (one of Rogers's adoption factors). Conversely, the more 'core' components your innovation has, the less complex it is to scale, but the less customisable it is for Value Consumers individual needs and preferences.

By establishing which components are core, modular or hackable, you will be able to assess how you will go about codifying the components for scalability.

EXERCISE ›

CORE, MODULAR, HACKABLE AND CODIFICATION

Determine what components of your innovation are core (the same everywhere), modular (you provide a choice of options), hackable (the Value Consumer can add their own components).

→ **API APPLICATION PROGRAMMING INTERFACE**

is a way of two or more computer applications communicating with each other and sharing data.

Solution Lifecycle

In creating your MVP, and in piloting your innovation, you will have been concentrating on whether the innovation works and whether people or organisations want it. In order to scale, however, you will need to ensure that the innovation has a fully worked-out solution lifecycle. By this we mean that you have fully mapped out and (where possible) tested how your innovation will be used and supported from beginning to the end of its life. Who will provide training if it is needed? How will technical support be provided? What happens if someone wants a refund or to return the product? What happens if an organisation wants to upgrade their package? If it is a physical product, how is it disposed of in an environmentally friendly manner? If it is a process or service innovation, how will you incorporate user feedback to improve the process or service in the future?

The best way to map this out is to use a solution lifecycle. There are a number of ways to do this, but we prefer a method that shows three perspectives:

▷ The consumer's perspective
▷ Your organisation's perspective
▷ Your partners' perspectives

EXERCISE ›
SOLUTION LIFECYCLE
How to map your solution journey.

→ **SOLUTION LIFECYCLE**

The Solution Lifecycle is mapping how the lifecycle of your innovation from the first stages of producing it, all the way to what happens to it at the end of it's useful life (e.g., recycling options for physical products).

DEFENSIBILITY: MAKING SURE YOUR INNOVATION IS 'RIGHTS READY'

How the intellectual property (IP) in your innovation is treated has a significant bearing on how your innovation scales and how value is captured. The treatment of IP is about whether you want to protect it or not, and if you do, how do you want to protect it. Your decision in this area will impact three key areas of scaling:

- *The **scaling pathway** you use is significantly affected by how you treat the IP created in your innovation, e.g., it will determine whether you can scale through licensing or franchising, or whether you create an open community to diffuse and build on the innovation.*

- *The **revenue models** open to you are also affected by how you treat your IP. For instance, open sourcing your innovation using a ➜ CREATIVE COMMONS LICENCE will often lead to the development of a complementary services model, where the revenue is based on technical support, consulting or training services.*

- ***Scaling speed** can also be influenced by how you treat your IP in terms of accessibility of the service. This is particularly true of models that require network effects to scale. In this model, the IP is retained by the company but the services provided are free or use a ➜ FREEMIUM MODEL. In this case, the IP can be protected but the service is opened out. This enables quick adoption which, if based on a network effects model, drives uptake and thereby scaling.*

This is just a start to the decision-making process. We strongly encourage you to seek legal advice when making your decision on the IP that has been created in your innovation.

➜ **CREATIVE COMMONS LICENSE**

A Creative Commons license is a way of opening up an item of intellectual property to a wide range of users and allowing them to spread it further and to make use of it provided there is suitable attribution to the source creator.

➜ **FREEMIUM MODEL**

A freemium model is a way of allowing potential adopters to try out a product or piece of software before committing to full use. Typically a piece of software will be usable in its basic form for free but if the user wishes for the full range of functions or to unlock key features then they have to pay a premium for this.

VIII SOLUTION

WHERE ARE WE NOW AND WHERE DO WE NEED TO BE?

Now you have gone through the key aspects of making your innovation truly scalable, it is time to assess where your innovation is at using the following 12 key questions – they'll help you assess the scalability of your solution.

IS YOUR INNOVATION SCALABLE? DON'T START THE JOURNEY WITHOUT CHECKING THIS OUT!

EXERCISE › SOLUTION SCALABILITY ASSESSMENT

Decide where you are currently placed and then decide on where you need to be to achieve your scale goal, i.e., where you need to be within the next 12–36 months. Score them 1–5 to indicate the level for each area. We have provided a space for any areas that we have not covered in this chapter that you think is a gap that needs to be plugged for your solution.

SCORING

- [1] We are nowhere on this
- [2] We have thought about it
- [3] We have a plan
- [4] We have an approach
- [5] We have the scalable approach

SECTION	CHECKLIST	Score Now	Score at Scale Goal	Gap
Proven — A clear value proposition	1 — How clear is your value proposition?			
Proven — Evidence of value	2 — How well tested is your innovation?			
Proven — Adoptable	3 — Relative advantage: Is your innovation better than its competition on the factors most important to consumers?			
Proven — Adoptable	4 — Compatibility: Does your innovation interact with the other elements around it seamlessly?			
Proven — Adoptable	5 — Complexity: How hard is it to understand and use your innovation?			

CHAP VIII — SOLUTION

Proven Adoptable	6 — Trialability: Can the buyer try before they buy?	☐	☐	☐
Proven Adoptable	7 — Observability: How easy is it to see the innovation and its value?	☐	☐	☐
Replicable Codification	8 — How replicable is your solution?	☐	☐	☐
Replicable Core, modular and hackable	9 — Does your innovation have the right level of customisability?	☐	☐	☐
Replicable Solution lifecycle	10 — Is your solution lifecycle developed?	☐	☐	☐
Defensible Rights ready	11 — Is your treatment of IP agreed and secure?	☐	☐	☐
Other	12 — Other outstanding gaps?	☐	☐	☐
Totals		☐	☐	☐

CHAPTER VIII — SUMMARY
WHAT YOU HAVE LEARNED IN THIS CHAPTER

In this chapter we have outlined how there are three critical areas where you need to stress test your innovation solution to see if it is ready to scale. These are to assess:

▷ **Is it proven?**
Does it have a clear and compelling value proposition, is it easily adoptable and do you have the right evidence to convince others in your Value Network that it adds value for them?

▷ **Is it replicable?**
Have the components of the innovation been codified, sorted into what is core, what is modular and what is hackable, and have you mapped out the solution lifecycle?

▷ **Is it defensible?**
Is your treatment of IP going to enable scale? Will it enable you to capture enough value?

CHAP IX

ORGANISATION

This chapter provides tools and guidance on how ready our organisation is to scale innovation. It focuses on three core elements: the organisational model, the capability model and the financial model. At the end of the chapter there will be a checklist for you to assess where you have gaps.

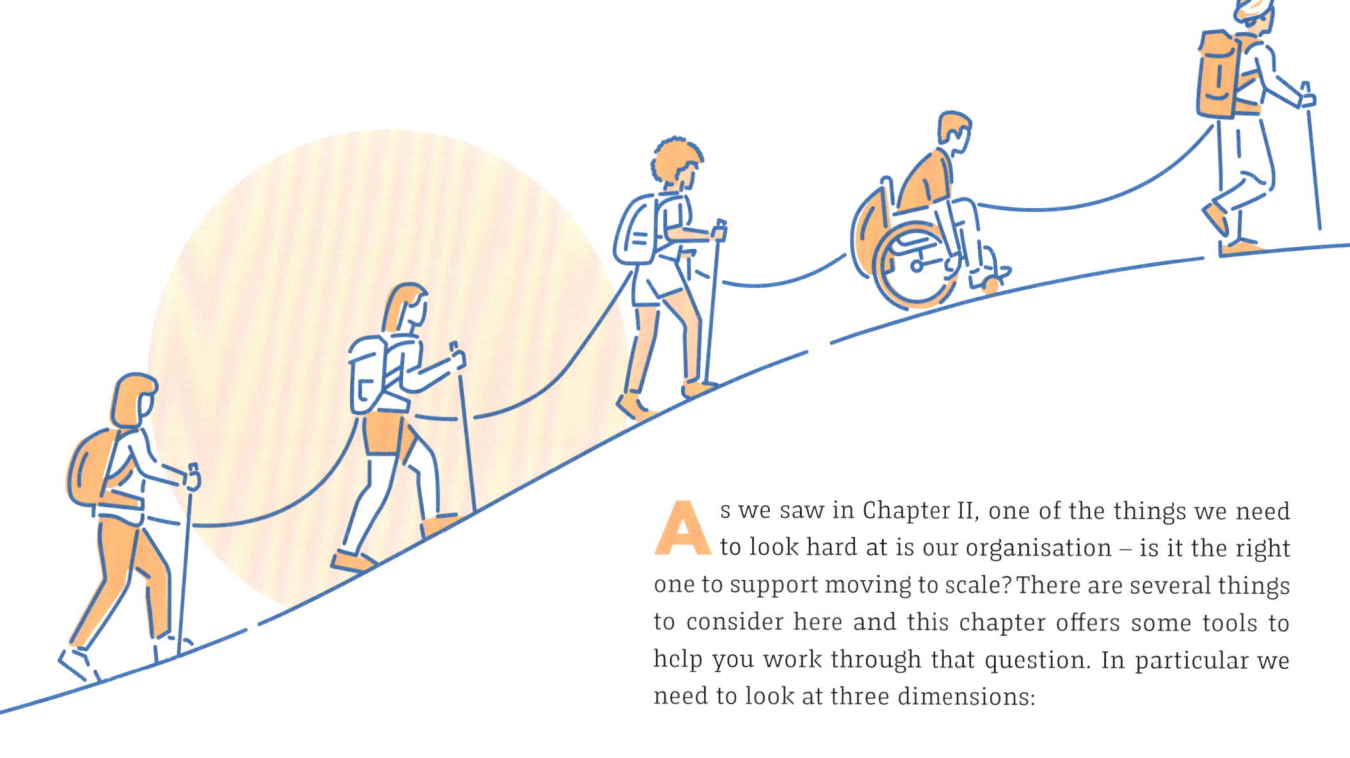

As we saw in Chapter II, one of the things we need to look hard at is our organisation – is it the right one to support moving to scale? There are several things to consider here and this chapter offers some tools to help you work through that question. In particular we need to look at three dimensions:

▷ Organisational model: How are you governed, structured and organised?
▷ Capability model: How do you manage your organisational culture and enable your people to make the transition to scale?
▷ Financial model: How do you create both a sustainable and scalable financial model?

SCALING THE INNOVATION MOUNTAIN REQUIRES AN ORGANISATION THAT IS CAPABLE OF MAKING THE SUMMIT.

TIP
To achieve Minimum Viable Bureaucracy requires design thinking and purposeful decision making.

ORGANISATIONAL MODEL

The organisational model you choose will need to particularly focus on your scaled operating model, how it is legally structured and governed, and how it facilitates scaling. You will also need to design a strategy for ensuring that, as you grow, you do not become overly bureaucratic. What we call aiming for minimum viable bureaucracy (MVB). Part of this approach is also to explore what you should be doing yourself as an organisation, and what you should have others do. This often changes as you go through a scaling journey, leading to that feeling of permeability and malleability of the organisation.

> **EXERCISE › REVIEW**
> Review your proposed organisational model and anticipated scale route to ensure there is a fit.

We recommend that you target two key areas of organisational life for systems and processes in order to ensure MVB: design and decisions.

- *Design: Identify the problem/need for each policy, process or system and ensure that it is truly needed. If it is, carry out an inclusive design criteria development exercise with the stakeholders (anyone who will use or be affected by the process or policy) and then design the process or policy and trial it before full implementation.*

- *Decisions: When making a decision on a new policy or process, go through a short list of questions to ensure that you do not create unnecessary bureaucracy. We suggest using the MVB checklist opposite as a good starting point whenever reviewing a new policy, process or system for implementation.*

ORGANISATION

> **CHECKLIST**
> **MINIMUM VIABLE BUREAU-CRACY (MVB)**
>
> - [ ] 1. Is this the simplest way of doing this?
> - [ ] 2. Is there a quicker way of doing this?
> - [ ] 3. Is there a cheaper way of doing this?
> - [ ] 4. Will this create a precedent or path dependency that might cause us problems in the future?
> - [ ] 5. Does this empower or disempower our staff?
> - [ ] 6. Will this increase organisational flexibility or increase organisational rigidity?

CAPABILITY MODEL

As we saw in Chapter II, we're looking to build capabilities which are VRIN (valuable, rare, inimitable and non-substitutable). We can either aim to build these directly or else access them through working with key complementors, something that the Liverpool Football Club case highlights (→ Chapter VI, p.136).

In the previous chapter we introduced exercises to identify the key components of your innovation, including the key activities that are carried out. It is a useful exercise to review these components and identify which are core capabilities and which aren't. For core capabilities it is often worth exploring how these can be potentially leveraged, in particular to create revenue streams. It is also helpful for identifying which activities might be best outsourced.

Insourcing and outsourcing

The ability to decide what is inside your organisation and what is outside of it is important since there are now so many options for outsourcing. These range from core administrative functions such as finance and HR,

TIP
Use the MVB checklist to ensure all new policies, processes and systems are not creating too much bureaucracy.

to crowdsourcing platforms (e.g., Fiverr or Amazon Mechanical Turk) for technical skills, to software development houses, to fully automated third-party and AI systems and processes to increase productivity. But outsourcing decisions should be driven by what you believe your core capabilities are now and what you believe they should be in the future as you scale.

TIP
AI productivity applications can reduce costs and increase capability for your organisation.

> **EXERCISE › CORE CAPABILITY FINDER**
> A tool to help you map your capabilities

Two key areas for building capabilities are your culture and your people.

Culture

We saw in Chapter II that culture can be seen as 'the way we do things round here' and a helpful tool for mapping it is the cultural web developed by Johnson and Scholes.

> **EXERCISE › CULTURAL WEB**
> A tool to help you map your organisation's culture.

People – pirates, privateers and petty officers

We also saw in Chapter II that there are several key roles which people can play, including pirates, privateers and petty officers.

You don't want your team to lose their entrepreneurial, pirate spark, but you need a way of engaging with the wider Value Network and their petty officers. So, you need to grow your privateers.

> **EXERCISE › PIRATES, PRIVATEERS AND PETTY OFFICERS**
> A tool to identify the roles being played by your team members.

CHAP IX — ORGANISATION

SCALING A MOUNTAIN RELIES ON HAVING GUIDES TO HELP YOU ALONG THE WAY – THAT'S THE KEY ROLE WHICH MENTORS PLAY.

Mentoring

Mentoring matters – building a network of people with experience who can provide an external, objective view on your plans. Mentoring is not technical support on a particular aspect of your scaling journey, such as digital strategy or marketing approaches. It is providing the helicopter view of the whole journey from a vantage point of having scaled the same or similar mountain, or from being a guide for teams scaling many mountains. Mentors need to be critical friends who will tell you things straight, show you the cliff you might fall over before you do. If you can't find an individual who can provide the helicopter view, then make sure you have enough advisers who can cover the whole view between them.

TIP
For many organisations you will need more than one revenue stream.

FINANCIAL MODEL

Your financial model is critical for scaling. It will determine whether you make it across the chasm or not. Accountants will look at your revenue and costs (in your profit and loss statement), your balance sheet and your cash flow. Scaling puts intense pressure on cash flow, so developing suitable cost and revenue models will help ensure that you are able to smooth out your cash flow so that you remain viable as you scale.

As you prepare to scale, it is worth spending time testing whether you have the most appropriate revenue model for the next stage of your journey.

> **EXERCISE ›**
> **REVENUE MODELS**
> We have prepared some ideas on revenue models as an exercise to download.

Cost models

The same is true for cost models – we need to ensure they're well developed. So how does yours look?

> **EXERCISE › COST-MINIMISATION MODELS**
> We have prepared some ideas on cost-minimisation models as an exercise to download.

IX ORGANISATION

FINANCIAL MODELS MATTER IN SCALING – IT'S ABOUT ENSURING REVENUE STREAMS TO SUPPORT THE NEXT STAGES ON WHAT IS GOING TO BE A COSTLY JOURNEY.

INVESTMENT AND DEBT

Many innovations and organisations can't get across the chasm/valley of death on earned revenue alone; investment is needed to make the journey. Investment can come in the form of equity, grants or even investing using debt through taking on loans. Always get solid financial advice. You don't want to give up too much equity or take on too much debt, but you also don't want to miss your chance at scaling. This is one area above all others that you need to make sure you get professional advice from a trusted source!

TIP

In their book *Innovation Accounting,* Esther Gons and Dan Toma explore some of the key metrics and approaches to innovation accounting:

Toma, D. & Gons, E. (2022). *Innovation Accounting: A Practical Guide For Measuring Your Innovation Ecosystem's Performance*. Amsterdam: BIS.

EXERCISE › ORGANISATION SCALABILITY ASSESSMENT

Here is a checklist of the key questions we ask intrapreneurs and entrepreneurs about their teams and organisations. As with the solution scale stress test in Chapter VIII, we use a five-level scoring approach.

You can score yourself before you read this chapter and then review it after you have read the chapter, or you can read the chapter and come back to create your scores. We have provided a space for any areas that we have not covered in this chapter that you think is a gap that needs to be plugged for your organisation.

SCORING

1. We are nowhere on this
2. We have thought about it
3. We have a plan
4. We have an approach
5. We have a scalable approach

Section	Checklist	Score Now	Score at Scale Goal	Gap
Organisation model	1 — **Structure:** Are you in the right legal structure and organisational model with the right governance mechanisms to scale?	☐	☐	☐
Organisation model	2 — **Systems and processes:** Do you have a defined approach to ensuring minimum viable bureaucracy as you grow?	☐	☐	☐
Organisation model	3 — **Scale route:** Does your organisational model fit with your anticipated scaling route?	☐	☐	☐
Capability model	4 — **Leadership:** How well set up are you to deal with any of the leadership team leaving?	☐	☐	☐

IX — ORGANISATION

Capability model	5 — **Team balance:** Have you got enough staff and are they diverse and balanced enough for scale?	☐	☐	☐
Capability model	6 — **Mentoring:** Do you have a mentor(s) who are able to provide advice on scaling?	☐	☐	☐
Capability model	7 — **Core capabilities:** Do you have the right functions insourced and outsourced for scale?	☐	☐	☐
Capability model	8 — **Culture:** Do you have a clear culture maintenance and building plan?	☐	☐	☐
Financial model	9 — **Revenue:** Have you identified the right revenue model mix?	☐	☐	☐
Financial model	10 — **Cost:** Do you have the right cost structure?	☐	☐	☐
Financial model	11 — **Investment/debt:** Will you have sufficient cash flow to reach your scale goal? If not, do you have an investment strategy?	☐	☐	☐
Other	12 — Other outstanding gaps?	☐	☐	☐
Totals		☐	☐	☐

CHAPTER IX — SUMMARY
WHAT YOU HAVE LEARNED IN THIS CHAPTER

In this chapter we have identified the three key organisational areas to consider when scaling.

▷ **Organisational model**
How are you governed, structured and organised?

▷ **Capability model**
How do you manage your organisational culture and enable your people to make the transition to scale?

▷ **Financial model**
How do you create both a sustainable and scalable financial model?

CHAP X

BOOKENDS

In this chapter we will take a look in more depth at each of the roles in the Value Network, highlighting key opportunities and challenges that the roles face, and provide a card for each role that you can use to build out the value roles. We will also look at different role combinations and what they can deliver.

BOOKEND ROLES

As we saw in Chapter IV, Bookends are where value is created, consumed and captured. This will be the primary category that you are focused on in the early days of your innovation, but they remain important throughout your scaling journey.

VALUE CONSUMER

If you are reading this book, you should have already piloted your innovation with your target Value Consumer group (whether individuals, organisations or governments) and addressed the key desirability risks, regarding whether this consumer group wants and is willing to pay for your innovation. (If you haven't reached this stage, then you need to go through this process before you can even think about scaling.)

TIP

We would recommend you read *Testing Business Ideas* by Bland and Osterwalder.

Bland, D.J. & Osterwalder, A. (2019). *Testing Business Ideas: A Field Guide for Rapid Experimentation*. Hoboken NJ: Wiley.

So, who are your target Value Consumers? (If you want a reminder of this role, look back to Chapter IV.)

> **EXERCISE › VALUE CONSUMERS**
> Create a list of all of your Value Consumers. Create a list of potential new Value Consumers as you scale.

TIP

It's worth going to the source and exploring Rogers's many valuable insights on adoption, drawn from his extensive synthesis of widely different innovations.

Value Consumer market sizing

Once you have a strong understanding of your Value Consumers, you need to identify which ones are customers (i.e., those paying for your innovation) and, when aggregated together, how large a market they are. This basic calculation will enable you to make quick decisions regarding whether the market is big enough to truly scale in. It will also highlight the size of operation you need to be planning for. Finally, it will enable you to estimate the break-even point based on projected costs and revenue.

This is particularly critical in ascertaining how much investment you might need to bridge the gap between revenue and costs when you hit the valley of death. We can use the simple distribution curve developed by Everett Rogers which we saw in Chapter II to help us here.

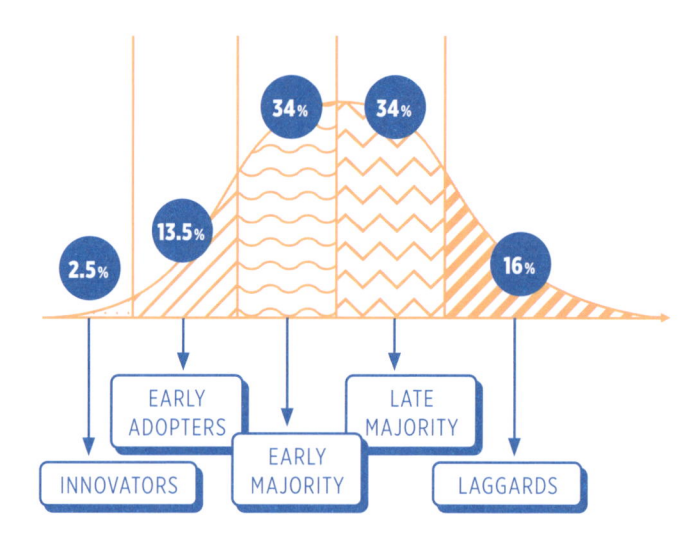

ROGERS'S ADOPTER DISTRIBUTION CURVE

2.5% INNOVATORS
13.5% EARLY ADOPTERS
34% EARLY MAJORITY
34% LATE MAJORITY
16% LAGGARDS

CHAP X — BOOKENDS

EXAMPLE › MARKET SIZING

Use this approach to explore your market sizing ideas. The table below gives an example of a rough market scaling estimate table.

INSTRUCTIONS

▷ Choose the geography/market you are sizing, e.g., India

▷ Research the size of the potential market and the current market for your product/service category

▷ Decide on what percentage of the market you believe you can gain as a market share when at full scale

This approach provides you with a good yardstick to know when you have entered the early majority (over 16% of your target market share), as well as some tangible figures to apply to your scaling vision.

MARKET SEGMENT	DESCRIPTION	NUMBER
Total potential market	All Value Consumers in your chosen geography/market	**10,000,000**
Total current market	Number of paying customers	**6,000,000**
Total target market share (e.g., 25 %)	The percentage of this market that you are aiming to reach	**1,500,000**
Target market needed to achieve scale	84 % of target market share (all the market except laggards) you are targeting	**1,260,000**
Innovator and early adopter market before reaching the early majority	16 % of target market share	**240,000**

Working with Value Consumers

As we saw in Chapter V (→ p.90), Value Networks and the roles entities play within them change over time. We can use this to our advantage: if we can imagine the ways in which roles might develop, we can create strategies to try and enable the more favourable configurations and strengthen our Value Network.

Below are the five most common role combinations for Value Consumers.

- *Consumer and creator:* Think about Lego's engagement with consumers as co-creators or giffgaff using customers as their first line of technical support (we saw both examples in Chapter V).

- *Consumer and captor:* The example of bottle recycling where in a number of countries a reward is offered to return a glass bottle, creating value capture for the consumer.

- *Consumer and cartographer:* Consumer rights groups can be strong Shapers of how much value is created through litigation and policy influencing.

- *Consumer and coordinator:* In the case of Tupperware, consumers hosted parties that brought consumers together with the opportunity to buy the product.

- *Consumer and conveyor:* Making customers carry out jobs traditionally done by other parts of the company or Value Network, such as airlines making you print off your own tickets.

TIP
Take another look at the cases we presented in Chapter VI – and try and map how value roles in their network changed over time.

EXERCISE ›
STRATEGIC MOVES

What strategic moves could be attempted with your Value Consumers?

Look again at your Value Consumers and think about how you might strategically develop their role to help strengthen your Value Network.

CHAP X — BOOKENDS

VALUE CREATOR

> SOMETIMES VALUE CREATION IS LIKE A RELAY RACE, THE BATON GETS PASSED ALONG TO OTHERS AS YOU MOVE ALONG THE SCALING JOURNEY.

EXERCISE ›
VALUE CREATORS

Create a list of all of your Value Creators.
Create a list of potential new Value Creators as you scale.
(If you want a reminder of this role, look back to Chapter IV).

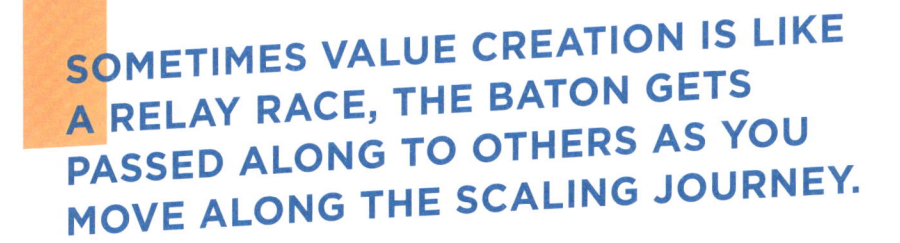

Working with Value Creators

As we saw in Chapter IV, early stage Value Creators often change as an innovation moves to scale. We have worked with innovations that have found the transitions from co-creators to other roles or no roles at all difficult, with a misunderstanding of roles as the transition to scale happens. This often leads to, at best, some bruised egos and broken relationships, and at worst law-suits and value destruction. So, pay careful attention to how you manage the transition of stakeholders who were playing creator roles, but are no longer needed in those roles for scaling.

TIP

The field of user-led innovation is rich with examples of people who have begun as frustrated consumers and gone on to become successful creators – 'user innovators'.

You can watch a video exploring this here:

In the transitions of the journey to scale, co-creators are not always dropped but are also placed in different roles. There are three roles that they can often move to:

- *Mover* roles such as a conveyor who supplies you

- *Shaper* roles such as a complementor who remains in the Value Network but you no longer need to partner with

- A *competitor* when you have not protected the IP either by mistake or design

Let's remind ourselves of some of the ways in which creator roles can shift.

- *Creator to captor:* Nearly all Value Creators are putting in their effort and support in order to receive some form of value in return.

- *Creator to conveyor*: Creators moving into the conveyor position. An example of this is Hilti who have moved beyond the manufacture of power tools into innovating their business model so that they are also a conveyor, selling tool fleet management where they provide access to tools when they are needed.

- *Creator to consumer:* Value Creators can use their own experience as consumers of their process innovations, for example Slack. During the process of creating an online game, they created a workflow and communications application. When the game they were creating failed to take off, they pivoted to commercialising the product that they had created for themselves.

- *Creator to cartographer:* In late-stage scaling, many creators try to move into the cartographer space. This can be by joining key industry bodies or government task forces and often goes beyond the role of lobbying and influencing because the creators are now involved in the policy- or law-making process.

CHAP X — BOOKENDS

> **EXERCISE ›**
> **STRATEGIC MOVES**
>
> What strategic moves could be attempted with your Value Creators?
>
> Look again at your Value Creators and think about how you might strategically develop their role to help strengthen your Value Network.

VALUE CAPTORS

Value capture is key in Value Network development. All the roles in your inner Value Network will require some kind of value capture. The most straightforward is financial – something that is the case for the value creator (as innovators, entre/intrapreneurs or investors) but is also the case for coordinators and conveyors in the Mover category. However, financial value is not the only type of value that different roles might want to capture. Understanding and delivering the type of value capture sought by the different roles is arguably the most important factor to ensure successful scaling.

TIP
Making sure 'everyone gets a pony' is critical for the scale journey.

PART 2   WORKING ON YOUR JOURNEY TO SCALE

Scaling is usually a journey of increasing the number of partnerships that you have, and this often equates to expanding the number of entities that are seeking value capture. Make sure that you understand the value capture needs of these new partners and are not offering or enabling value that they aren't interested in. (If you want a reminder of this role, look back to Chapter IV.)

TYPES OF VALUE
stakeholders might want to capture

brand
staff well-being
knowledge
positioning
lower cost
know-how
economies of scale
customer retention
expanded networks
new market expansion
staff retention
geographical expansion

EXERCISE › VALUE CAPTORS
Create a list of all of your existing Value Captors. Create a list of potential new Value Captors as you scale.

Working with Value Captors

Let's remind ourselves of some of the ways in which captor roles can shift:

- *Captor to creator:* *This might be a passive investor who decides to get more active. Sean Parker was an early investor in Spotify but helped enhance the core offering with his advice and experience, effectively taking a creator role.*

- *Captor to cartographer:* *How much value can be captured is often determined by the influence over the rules for the Value Network and wider ecosystem, such as self-regulating markets where 'cartels' control the value capture, e.g., sports bodies such as the NBA and English Premier League.*

- *Captor to coordinator:* *For many Value Networks, captors will often seek to create a two-sided platform as value capture comes from both creator and consumer, such as Amazon's move into this area.*

> **EXERCISE ›**
> **STRATEGIC MOVES**
> Look again at your Value Captors and think about how you might strategically develop their role to help strengthen your Value Network.

WHERE ARE WE NOW AND WHERE DO WE NEED TO BE?

Rank where you think your innovation is now. We provide the 9 key questions that will assess how scale-ready your Bookends are.

PART 2   WORKING ON YOUR JOURNEY TO SCALE

EXERCISE › BOOKENDS SCALABILITY ASSESSMENT

Decide where you are currently placed and then decide on where you need to be to achieve your scale goal, i.e., where you need to be within the next 12–36 months. Score them 1–5 to indicate the level for each area.

You can score yourself before you read this chapter and then review it after you have read the chapter, or you can read the chapter and come back to create your scores. We have provided a space for any areas that we have not covered in this chapter that you think is a gap that needs to be plugged for the Bookends.

SCORING

[1] We are nowhere on this

[2] We have thought about it

[3] We have a plan

[4] We have a tested approach

[5] We have a scalable approach

SECTION	CHECKLIST	Score Now	Score at Scale Goal	Gap
Value Creators	**1** — Do you know how existing value creation roles will change as you scale?	☐	☐	☐
Value Creators	**2** — Do you need new Value Creators as you scale?	☐	☐	☐
Value Consumers	**3** — Do you know how existing Value Consumer roles will change as you scale?	☐	☐	☐
Value Consumers	**4** — Do you know how many new Value Consumers you are aiming to reach for your scale goal?	☐	☐	☐

BOOKENDS

Value Consumers	**5** — Do you know how many new Value Consumers you aim to reach when you are at full scale (your scale vision)?	☐	☐	☐
Value Captors	**6** — Do you know how existing value capture role needs will change as you scale?	☐	☐	☐
Value Captors	**7** — Will there be new entities that will need to capture value?	☐	☐	☐
Value Captors	**8** — Can all the entities who are seeking to capture value be able to capture the value that they are looking for?	☐	☐	☐
Other	**9** — Other outstanding gaps?	☐	☐	☐
Totals		☐	☐	☐

CHAPTER X — SUMMARY
WHAT YOU HAVE LEARNED IN THIS CHAPTER

▷ Each of the bookend value roles are likely to be the ones that you had entities playing from the earliest days of your innovation.

▷ As you move to scale you will find that a number of entities in your Value Network will change roles. It is particularly important to be mindful of changes in the creator and captor roles as you can often store up problems ahead if you do not think through the implications of the changes that will need to be made, and how you make them.

CHAP XI

MOVERS

In this chapter we will take a look in more depth at each of the roles in the Mover category of the Value Network, highlighting key opportunities and challenges that the roles face, and provide a checklist for each role that you can use to identify which entities are playing each role. We will also look at different role combinations and what they can deliver.

MOVER ROLES

Movers are roles that often change as you start scaling. The two most common changes are: the need to adjust Movers in order to reach different markets; and for Value Creators to take on mover roles themselves, both upstream and downstream.

If you need a quick reminder of how to identify the differences between the three types of Movers – channel, conveyor or co-ordinator – refer back to our helpful chart in Chapter IV (→ p.80).

VALUE CHANNELS

Channels are ways of moving value either upstream through a supply chain, or downstream to a consumer. The value might be in the form of a product or service, or by just increasing consumers' knowledge of your product or service, such as through advertising on a website.

For physical products, think UPS, DPD or a local delivery driver as examples of a channel. For digital services, think about internet service providers. For advertising, think newspapers, magazines, billboards and websites. (If you want a reminder of this role, look back to Chapter IV.)

Channels do not add value to the product or service itself. They can increase efficiency, reduce friction and potentially reduce cost, so although this can benefit the consumer, it is not changing the value derived from the use of the innovation itself. This means that the relationship with them is almost always transactional and they are generally only concerned with financial payment as their form of value capture.

VALUE CHANNEL
A Mover that does not add value to the innovation itself.

CREATOR — Level of Value → CHANNEL — Level of Value → CONSUMER

However, it would be wrong to see channels as just a commodity business that doesn't have the potential to scale. Look back at the case of Malcolm McLean (Chapter VI) and the way he moved from being a channel (running a trucking business) to changing the world through the introduction of containerisation!

> **EXERCISE ›**
> **VALUE CHANNELS**
> Create a list of all of your existing Value Channels.
> Create a list of potential new Value Channels as you scale.

WORKING WITH VALUE CHANNELS

Let's remind ourselves of some of the ways in which channel roles can shift.

Channels can often be used as a springboard for moving into other roles. These are the common moves that are played.

- *Channel to conveyor: Netflix started out as barely more than a channel, posting DVDs to Value Consumers. However, it managed to transition to a conveyor when it added value by allowing consumers to keep the DVDs for as long as they liked and creating an algorithm to guide them to movies they might like.*

- *Channel and coordinator: Amazon started as a channel (similar to Netflix) but instead of posting videos, they sold books online. They quickly expanded from a bookseller to a marketplace, bringing customers and sellers together onto the world's biggest platform.*

- *Channel and competitor: The rise in the white labelling of products has seen a number of channels in the retail space start competing with creators who are using them by carrying their own brand versions of the same products.*

TIP

There's a useful blog here which charts the history of Amazon and its moves from simply replacing a physical bookselling channel to the sophisticated online retailing platform it now represents:

> **EXERCISE ›**
> **STRATEGIC MOVES**
> Look again at your Value Channels and think about how you might strategically develop their role to help strengthen your Value Network.

VALUE CONVEYOR

Value Conveyors can be the key to success or failure for many innovations as they can create or destroy the value of the innovation itself. Value Conveyors play a critical role in the amount of value created by your product or service.

VALUE CONVEYOR

Conveyors increase the value of the innovation as they supply or move components of the innovation.

CREATOR → Level of Value → CONVEYOR → Level of Value → CONSUMER

MOVERS

This is what makes them distinct from channels that, at best, can only impact the delivery of the innovation, not the innovation itself. (If you want a reminder of this role, look back to Chapter IV.)

> **EXERCISE ›**
> **VALUE CONVEYORS**
> Create a list of all of your existing Value Conveyors. Create a list of potential new Value Conveyors as you scale.

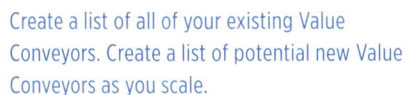

Working with Value Conveyors

As with channels, conveyors can take on other roles within the Value Network. Let's remind ourselves of some of the ways in which conveyor roles can shift.

- *Conveyor to creator*: *Conveyors by definition are creating value, but to someone else's innovation. They can also move directly into the creator space by moving up or down the supply chain to become the main creator of a product or service. Netflix, again, is an example of this, where they have moved from being a content streamer to a content producer.*

- *Conveyor to competitor:* *The conveyor to creator move also means that conveyors can become competitors for creators and vice versa when creators move into spaces formerly occupied by conveyors to compete with them. Viewed from Intel's vantage point, this is what Apple did when they moved from purchasing their chips from intel to making their own.*

- *Conveyor plus captor:* *Conveyors by definition are adding value to an innovation; they therefore need to capture value. Often this will be solely financial, but there may be other types of value that are important to them. An example of this is conveyors of digital public goods, such as KoboToolbox, which is a digital data-gathering conveyor that adds value to Open Data Kit but is also seeking to capture value by collecting social impact data for itself.*

TIP

The pioneering work of George Washington Carver in spreading and scaling agricultural innovations in the United States provides an excellent example of his role as conveyor; his subsequent work on crops like peanuts helped establish him as a creator. You can read more about this here:

> **EXERCISE ›**
> **STRATEGIC MOVES**
> Look again at your Value Conveyors and think about how you might strategically develop their role to help strengthen your Value Network.

VALUE COORDINATORS

Value Coordinators play a key role in bringing players in the ecosystem together and, as we have seen, moving to create a platform or similar coordination arrangement is a key way of managing the move to significant scale – as the Netflix, Spotify and Amazon examples demonstrate. (If you want a reminder of this role, look back to Chapter IV.)

VALUE COORDINATOR

Value Coordinators should add value for the Value Creators and Value Consumers.

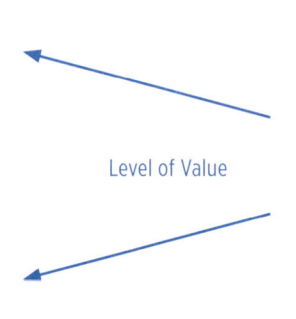

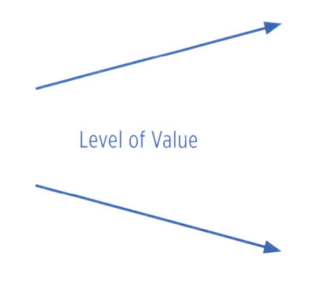

CREATOR — Level of Value — COORDINATOR — Level of Value — CONSUMER

MOVERS

> **EXERCISE › VALUE COORDINATORS**
>
> Create a list of all of your existing Value Coordinators.
> Create a list of potential new Value Coordinators as you scale.

Working with Value Coordinators

Let's remind ourselves of some of the ways in which coordinator roles can shift.

- *Coordinator to channel to creator:* Department stores are coordinators and not just channels because they house concessions – almost like mini-shops for different brands – thereby coordinating Value Creators with Value Consumers. However, they also use white labelling to create their own products that are sold as their own products, competing with the other brands they stock.

- *Coordinator to cartographer:* Coordinators often have significant power over the market, either indirectly through setting standards for industries, or through significant lobbying power with legislators.

- *Coordinator and complementor:* Coordinators will often bundle complementor products and services together. For example, airlines will bundle complementors of flight, hotel, travel insurance and car hire together as offers during the purchasing process.

> **EXERCISE › STRATEGIC MOVES**
>
> Look again at your Value Conveyors and think about how you might strategically develop their role to help strengthen your Value Network.

WHERE ARE WE NOW AND WHERE DO WE NEED TO BE?

Rank where you think your innovation is now. Here are 10 key questions that will assess how scaleready your Movers are.

TIP
This example of Ryanair highlights the ways in which coordinators can bundle other complementary services:

PART 2   WORKING ON YOUR JOURNEY TO SCALE

EXERCISE › MOVERS SCALABILITY ASSESSMENT

For Movers, rank where you think your innovation is now. Decide where you are currently placed, and then decide on where you need to be to achieve your scale goal, i.e., where you need to be within the next 12–36 months. Score them 1–5 to indicate the level for each area. You may use just one type of Mover, or use two or more types. The important thing is to have a strategy for how you will scale through your Movers.

You can score yourself before you read this chapter and then review it after you have read the chapter, or you can read the chapter and come back to create your scores. Remember, you probably won't use all of the Mover roles to scale. Just complete the ones that are relevant for you.

We have provided a space for any areas that we have not covered in this chapter that you think is a gap that needs to be plugged for the Movers.

SCORING

1. We are nowhere on this
2. We have thought about it
3. We have a plan
4. We have a tested approach
5. We have a scalable approach

SECTION	CHECKLIST	Score Now	Score at Scale Goal	Gap
Value Channels	1 — Are our current channels the right ones for scaling?	☐	☐	☐
Value Channels	2 — Should we take on a channel role?	☐	☐	☐
Value Conveyors	3 — Are our current conveyors the right ones for scaling?	☐	☐	☐

XI CHAP — MOVERS

Value Conveyors	4 — Should we take on a conveyor role upstream?	☐	☐	☐
Value Conveyors	5 — Should we take on a conveyor role downstream?	☐	☐	☐
Value Conveyors	6 — Are our conveyors capturing the right amount of value?	☐	☐	☐
Value Coordinator	7 — Is our coordinator the right one for scaling?	☐	☐	☐
Value Coordinator	8 — Are our coordinators capturing the right amount of value?	☐	☐	☐
Value Coordinator	9 — Should we take on a coordinator role?	☐	☐	☐
Other	10 — Any other gaps?	☐	☐	☐
Totals		☐	☐	☐

CHAPTER XI — SUMMARY
WHAT YOU HAVE LEARNED IN THIS CHAPTER

▷ This chapter has shown the different Mover roles and why they are so important for scaling. It has also provided examples of how Movers can actually become the dominant entities in a Value Network.

▷ Strategies for Movers are likely to change significantly as you start to scale. Decisions about whether you need to take on a Mover role, either through vertical integration to become a conveyor or by becoming a coordinator or channel. Identifying what type of Movers you will use and whether they are able to reach your Value Consumers at scale is critical.

CHAP XII

SHAPERS

Shapers control the level of value within a network. In this chapter we explore shaper roles, providing examples and key questions that you need to think through.

SHAPER ROLES

COMPLEMENTORS

Entities that influence the value of your innovation

Complementors come in different shapes and sizes; they can be an entity that is a piece of physical or digital infrastructure, they can be former competitors or part-time competitors (co-opetition), they can be producing goods or services that your innovation relies on or leverages. They can be arranged and behave in multiple ways.

Nearly all products and services require some form of complementors to be in place for them to maximise the value they create for Value Consumers. (If you want a reminder of this role, look back to Chapter IV.)

> **EXERCISE › VALUE COMPLEMENTORS**
>
> Create a list of all of your existing Value Complementors
> Create a list of potential new Value Complementors as you scale.

WORKING WITH VALUE COMPLEMENTORS

Let's remind ourselves of some of the ways in which complementor roles can shift.

- *Complementor to co-creator:* Complementors are often creators in their own right for their own innovative products and services. But they can also become creators that collaborate with you on your innovation.

- *Complementor to conveyor:* Building an API to another app is leveraging a complementor, but signing an agreement with that app to more formally integrate moves them to a conveyor.

- *Complementor to competitor:* Complementors can often become competitors as they expand their offering, developing value propositions that are directly competing with you own innovation.

> **EXERCISE ›**
> **STRATEGIC MOVES**
>
> Look again at your Value Complementors and think about how you might strategically develop their role to help strengthen your Value Network.

TIP
Complementors can be infrastructure, such as internet access, or other organisations providing products or services your innovation relies upon.

COMPLEMENTORS ENHANCE THE VALUE OF YOUR INNOVATION FOR VALUE CONSUMERS. THEY ARE OFTEN CRITICAL TO YOUR SCALE SUCCESS.

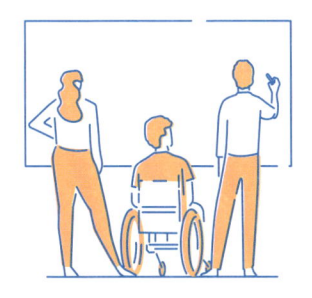

CARTOGRAPHERS

Entities that determine the boundaries and amount of value that is possible within a market

There are entities that impact every Value Network by determining the rules of the game in that market. They can be legal, social, technological or economic. (If you want a reminder of this role, look back to Chapter IV.)

> **EXERCISE › VALUE CARTOGRAPHERS**
>
> Create a list of all of your existing Value Cartographers. Create a list of potential new Value Cartographers as you scale.

Let's remind ourselves of some of the ways in which cartographer roles can shift.

- *Cartographer and complementor*: Cartographers are often responsible for public goods such as infrastructure, which are complementors. An example of this is road infrastructure that enables Movers to carry out their roles.

- *Cartographer to conveyor*: Cartographers may be part of the delivery of your solution, e.g., education technology through schools.

- *Cartographer to Value Consumer*: Cartographers may well be your Value Consumers, e.g., diagnostic machinery for hospitals purchased by the health ministry.

- *Cartographer to creator*: Cartographers can be part of the creation process, such as unions being part of the design process for a new service innovation.

TIP
Cartographers can be official, like regulators, or unofficial, like 'gatekeepers' to a community you are trying to reach.

> **EXERCISE ›**
> **STRATEGIC MOVES**
>
> Look again at your Value Cartographers and think about how you might strategically develop their role to help strengthen your Value Network.

Innovation takes place in a competitive arena with different entities looking to increase their market share against others. Competition can come from many directions, so it's important to map your Value Competitors and where possible explore ways in which you might work with them to draw them into alignment with your own goals – so-called 'co-opetition'.

TIP
Remember one of the best ways to deal with competitors can be to collaborate with them. Co-opetition can be a key to scaling.

COMPETITORS
Entities with similar value offerings to you for the same groups, or rivals for resources

> **EXERCISE ›**
> **VALUE COMPETITORS**
>
> Create a list of all of your existing Value Competitors.
> Create a list of potential new Value Competitors as you scale.

CHAP XII — SHAPERS

WORKING WITH VALUE COMPETITORS

Let's remind ourselves of some of the way in which cartographer roles can shift.

- *Competitor to creator:* The Covid-19 pandemic closed down Nascar racing, so they turned to an online competitor, iRacing, to produce a simulated version of its race schedule as part of a successful joint venture.

- *Competitor to coordinator:* Microsoft Azure services provides a marketplace for many software products and services that could be considered as competitors to Microsoft.

- *Competitor to cartographer:* Competitors often try to influence and become part of the cartographer group through gaining positions within government committees or industry umbrella organisations in order to influence rulings and regulations in their favour.

EXERCISE ›
STRATEGIC MOVES

Look again at your Value Competitors and think about how you might strategically develop their role to help strengthen your Value Network.

WHERE ARE WE NOW AND WHERE DO WE NEED TO BE?

Use these 13 questions to help assess how scale ready you are in respect of shapers.

TIP
Competitors are entities who are competing with you for staff, contracts, suppliers and other resources.

PART 2   WORKING ON YOUR JOURNEY TO SCALE

EXERCISE › SHAPERS SCALABILITY ASSESSMENT

For Shapers, rank where you think your innovation is now. Decide where you are currently placed, and then decide on where you need to be to achieve your scale goal, i.e., where you need to be within the next 12–36 months. Score them 1–5 to indicate the level for each area. The important thing is to have a strategy for how you will scale through your Shapers.

You can score yourself before you read this chapter and then review it after you have read the chapter, or you can read the chapter and come back to create your scores. We have provided a space for any areas that we have not covered in this chapter that you think is a gap that needs to be plugged for the Shapers.

SCORING

- [1] We are nowhere on this
- [2] We have thought about it
- [3] We have a plan
- [4] We have a tested approach
- [5] We have a scalable approach

SECTION	CHECKLIST	Score Now	Score at Scale Goal	Gap
Value Competitors	1 — We have a strong understanding of each of our competitors and their offerings?	☐	☐	☐
Value Competitors	2 — Strength vs. direct competitors	☐	☐	☐
Value Competitors	3 — Strength vs. indirect competitors	☐	☐	☐
Value Competitors	4 — Strength vs. business as usual	☐	☐	☐

XII — SHAPERS

Value Competitors	**5** — Strength vs. resource competitors	☐	☐	☐
Value Competitors	**6** — Ability to cooperate with or nullify competitors	☐	☐	☐
Value Cartographers	**7** — We know who the cartographers are as we move to scale	☐	☐	☐
Value Cartographers	**8** — The cartographers are supportive of our innovation scaling	☐	☐	☐
Value Cartographers	**9** — We have good access to inform and influence our key cartographers	☐	☐	☐
Value Complementors	**10** — We know who our complementors are	☐	☐	☐
Value Complementors	**11** — Our complementors are present in the markets we are seeking to scale in	☐	☐	☐
Value Complementors	**12** — We have the right combination of complementors for scale	☐	☐	☐
Other	**13** — Any other gaps?	☐	☐	☐
Totals		☐	☐	☐

CHAPTER XII — SUMMARY
WHAT YOU HAVE LEARNED IN THIS CHAPTER

▷ Shapers have significant control over how much value can be created, moved, consumed and captured by a Value Network.

▷ In this chapter we have seen that it is more than just cartographers who do this, but also competitors and complementors.

▷ As you scale, you will need to monitor the entities playing these roles, and are likely to increasingly engage with them directly, potentially bringing them into your Inner Value Network.

CHAP XIII
DEVELOPING VALUE NETWORKS

This chapter explores the steps to create a strategy around your Value Network. Firstly, identify and define the entities in your Value Network. Secondly, visualise your Value Network entities on our Value Network map, identifying who is in your IVN and OVN. Thirdly, create an action plan for each entity and finally, establish how to manage your IVN, and monitor and influence your OVN.

SCALING VALUE IS A MULTIPLAYER GAME IN THE FORM OF A VALUE NETWORK.

Mapping your Value Network then managing your Inner Value Network (IVN) and monitoring and influencing your Outer Value Network (OVN) is the key to scale. We use a four-step model to create a comprehensive approach to leveraging your Value Network to reach scale.

STEP 1 — IDENTIFY

In this step you will identify each entity that is needed for the next stage of your scale journey then identify what roles they will be required to play.

> **EXERCISE › IDENTIFY ROLES**
>
> List every entity that is required for you to take the next step in your scale journey. Remember, entities are not necessarily just people or organisations, but can also be infrastructure and technologies. Make sure you are exhaustive and capture all the entities.

Define

Once you have a list, use the Value Role Cards to define each entity's role(s). The value role cards are designed to enable you to capture the primary and secondary roles for each entity in your Value Network. They also enable you to identify the wants and needs of each stakeholder and articulate how they will be met.

In order to manage and monitor entities effectively, you must assign an entity a primary role. This is the most mission critical role for enabling your innovation or business to scale. When you have any conflict in how you relate to this entity, it will be the primary role that takes priority for decision making.

Using our scaling value role cards, pick one card per entity. Then, on the front of the card:

- ▷ Note the primary role
- ▷ Note any secondary roles

Then on the back of the card:

- ▷ Highlight each role the entity is playing; identify their wants and needs and then how you can meet them

You should now have a hand of cards that clearly indicate the primary role of each entity and their secondary roles.

MOST ENTITIES IN A VALUE NETWORK WILL PLAY MULTIPLE ROLES AT ONCE.

XIII CHAP — DEVELOPING VALUE NETWORKS

217

VALUE ROLE CARD

Value role card for an entity whose primary role is a Value Creator

VALUE CREATOR BOOKEND — PRIMARY ROLE

SECONDARY ROLES

BOOKENDS:
- CREATOR
- CAPTOR
- CONSUMER

MOVERS:
- CONVEYOR
- COORDINATOR
- CHANNEL

SHAPERS:
- COMPETITOR
- CARTOGRAPHER
- COMPLEMENTOR

BOOKENDS
- CREATOR
- CAPTOR
- CONSUMER

Wants & Needs

How we will meet them

MOVERS
- CONVEYOR
- COORDINATOR
- CHANNEL

Wants & Needs

How we will meet them

SHAPERS
- COMPETITOR
- CARTOGRAPHER
- COMPLEMENTOR

Wants & Needs

How we will meet them

STEP 2 — VISUALISE

The next step is to visualise how complex your Value Network will be to manage and monitor. We do this by using the Value Network map – a Venn diagram that shows:

▷ Whether an entity should be in your IVN or OVN
▷ What category or categories each entity sits in

For each entity card, place it in the most suitable place. If you do not need any type of partnership with them, they will belong in the Outer Value Network. For these entities, place them in the corresponding part of the map, e.g.; if their role is a bookend role, place them in the OVN Bookends area.

If you need some form of partnership with them, they will be in the IVN, which means that they should be placed within the Venn diagram circles. Where they are positioned within the Venn diagram will depend on how many roles in different categories they have. If it is in one category, you put it in the relevant category area where there aren't any overlaps. If it has roles in two categories, place it in the areas where the two circles for those categories overlap. If the entity will need to play roles in all three categories, place the card in the middle of the Venn diagram where all three circles overlap.

TIP
You can add lines to show connections between value role cards to show which entities have relationships with each other.

USE THE VALUE NETWORK MAP TO VISUALISE THE STRUCTURE OF YOUR VALUE NETWORK THAT IS NEEDED FOR SCALING YOUR INNOVATION.

XIII CHAP — DEVELOPING VALUE NETWORKS

VALUE NETWORK MAP

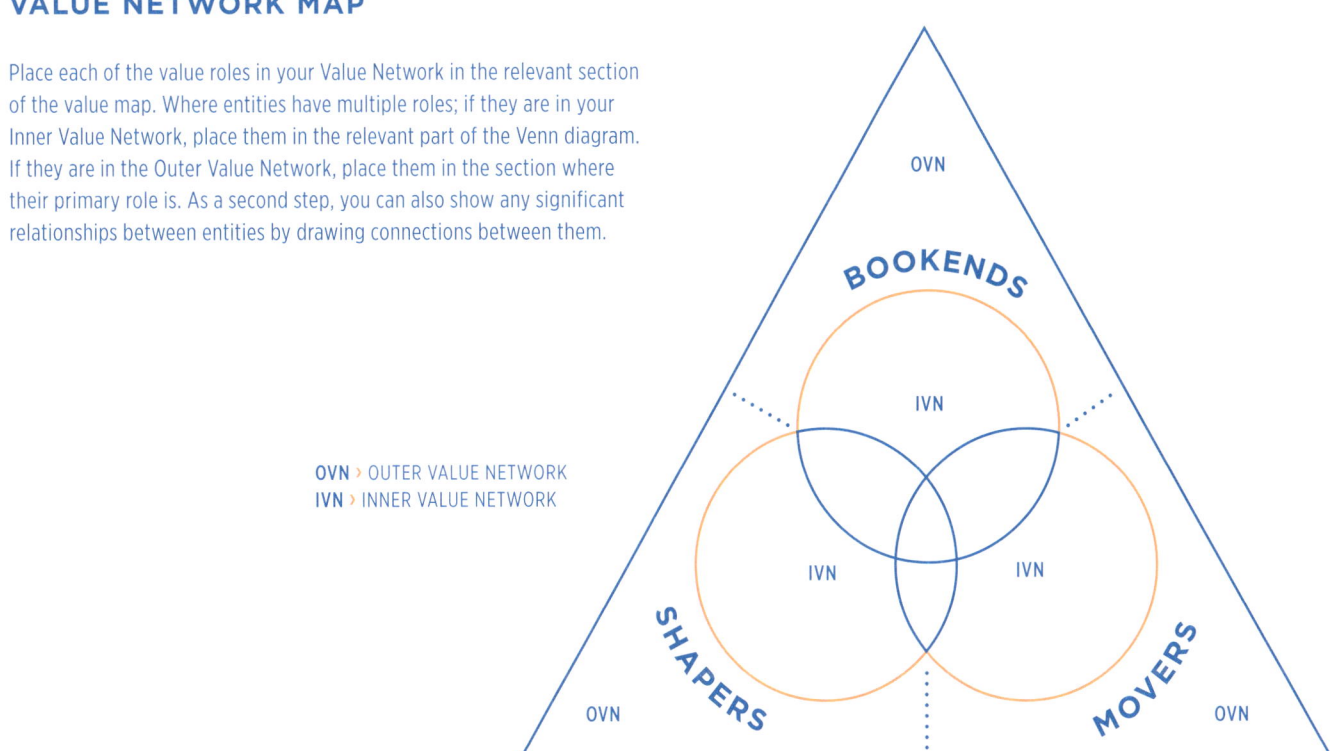

Place each of the value roles in your Value Network in the relevant section of the value map. Where entities have multiple roles; if they are in your Inner Value Network, place them in the relevant part of the Venn diagram. If they are in the Outer Value Network, place them in the section where their primary role is. As a second step, you can also show any significant relationships between entities by drawing connections between them.

OVN > OUTER VALUE NETWORK
IVN > INNER VALUE NETWORK

BOOKENDS
SHAPERS
MOVERS

OVN / IVN

MOVING FROM OVN TO IVN

An example of the movement of entities from the outer to Inner Value Network is Quality Teaching and Learning (QTL), an education innovation in Lebanon. The innovation started in the informal education sector, but it was clear that it would require Lebanon's Ministry of Education (MoE) to adopt it for it to truly scale across the country. When the innovation was being piloted, the MoE was part of the Outer Value Network, playing the role of Value Cartographer as they set the educational standards for the country and are the gatekeepers to working with head teachers and schools.

The innovation team needed to build a relationship with the MoE in order to have the innovation adopted within the formal school system. They needed to move the MoE from the OVN to the IVN and needed them to take on three more roles as well as their role as a cartographer. The first was as a Value Creator by working with the MoE (in collaboration with the Lebanese University) to create a training manual for teachers on the innovation. They then needed the MoE to become a Value Conveyor by training the teachers and instructing them to use the innovation in their teaching. Finally, the MoE was to be a consumer as they adopted the innovation across the education system.

By the end of the scaling process the MoE was in all three categories

- BOOKENDS → A CREATOR AND CONSUMER
- MOVERS → A CONVEYOR
- SHAPERS → A CARTOGRAPHER

Once you have done this, take a step back and look over the Value Network map. The more cards that you have in the overlap areas between categories, the more complex your IVN will be to manage. What tends to happen is that the further along the scale journey you are, the more of the entities that used to be in the OVN need to be brought into your IVN, as you build connections with them, making your IVN more populated and complex as you move along your scaling journey.

THE FURTHER ALONG YOUR SCALING JOURNEY, THE MORE ENTITIES ARE LIKELY TO MOVE FROM YOUR OVN TO IVN.

CHAP XIII — DEVELOPING VALUE NETWORKS

STEP 3 — ACTION

Now you have mapped the Value Network out, you have an understanding of its complexity and where you may need to move each entity to. The next step is to put together an action plan for each entity. Use the action planner below to highlight key actions to be taken with each entity.

First list your entities in the left-hand column. Then use a Post-it note or write directly onto the table to indicate what the key actions are under each of the roles that the entity plays. You will have this from the role card you have completed which will outline what their wants and needs are, and what you (or another entity in the Value Network) need to provide for them. Then, in the final two columns, note whether they are in your inner or outer Value Network and how you will monitor, or manage them.

Completing this table will provide you with a top-line action plan for your Value Network. It is also a chance to step back and review the following questions:

- Are there any roles that we should be moving into as we scale?

- Are there any roles we need to move out of in order to scale?

- Are there any roles that are missing an entity?

- Do we have duplication of entities in any of the roles and can this be rationalised?

- Can each of those entities deliver the roles that we want them to play at the scale we want to achieve in the next stage of our scale journey?

- Are there any entities that are not capturing value from their engagement in the Value Network? If so: Do they need to? What value are they seeking? Can it be provided?

TIP
If you are an intrapreneurial team, you may want to also use the role cards for mapping some of your key internal stakeholders and entities!

EXERCISE ›
VALUE NETWORK ACTION PLANNER

This table is to develop an action plan for each entity in your Value Network. List your entities in the left-hand 'Entity' column. Then in each cell that relates to their role/s, write what the key actions you need to take in order for them to enable you to scale.

Once you have done this, identify whether they will be in your Inner, or Outer Value Network, and outline what the key actions are in relation to this (e.g., need to move them from the Outer Value Network to Inner Value Network and sign a partnering agreement).

Finally, take a step back and identify where there are gaps in roles being played, and if these need to be filled. Also, ensure that you list your own organisation as an entity, as you may well need to change roles in the next stage of your scaling journey.

Entity	Bookends		
	CREATOR	CAPTOR	CONSUMER

DEVELOPING VALUE NETWORKS

Movers			Shapers			Value Network	
CONVEYOR	COORDINATOR	CHANNEL	COMPETITOR	CARTOGRAPHER	COMPLEMENTOR	INNER VALUE NETWORK	OUTER VALUE NETWORK

STEP 4 — MANAGING AND MONITORING

You have now got a good idea of what your Value Network needs to look like for the next stage of your scaling journey. The next step is to work out how you will manage your IVN and monitor your OVN.

Managing your IVN

For your IVN you need to work out what the structure and relationships should be. We provide a guide to some of the most common types of structure here. You may find that you need to combine a number of them or create a hybrid.

ACKNOWLEDGEMENT

A lot of this information is based on Michelle Halse's work on partnership typologies.

DETERMINE WHAT THE RIGHT STRUCTURE FOR YOU INNER VALUE NETWORK NEEDS TO BE TO SUPPORT SCALING.

SIMPLE
INNER VALUE NETWORKS

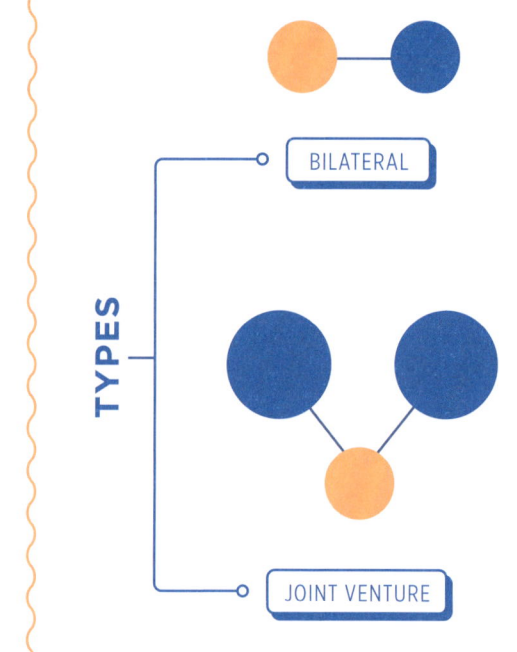

COMMON IVN STRUCTURES

TYPES
- BILATERAL
- JOINT VENTURE

Bilateral: A partnership with one other entity.
Joint Venture: Two or more partners create a new vehicle to scale the innovation.

XIII — DEVELOPING VALUE NETWORKS

CENTRALISED
INNER VALUE NETWORKS

TYPES
- BACKBONE
- HUB AND SPOKE
- LEAD AGENCY

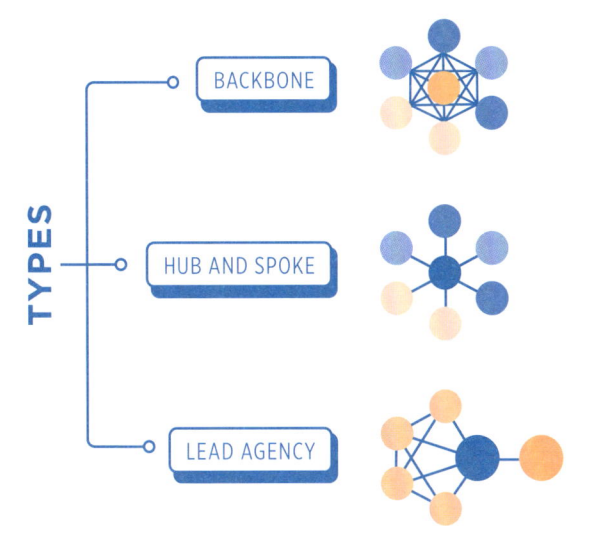

Backbone: A single organisation that supports the network for others, housing key functions, while the other partners still hold relationships with each other.

Hub and Spoke: One entity has individual partnerships with each partner, but the other partners don't have independent relationships with each other.

Lead Agency: For multistakeholder partnerships where there is a lead agency that is the 'primary' entity and then sub-contracts, sub-grants or manages other partners.

DECENTRALISED
INNER VALUE NETWORKS

TYPES
- STRUCTURED NETWORK
- UNSTRUCTURED NETWORK

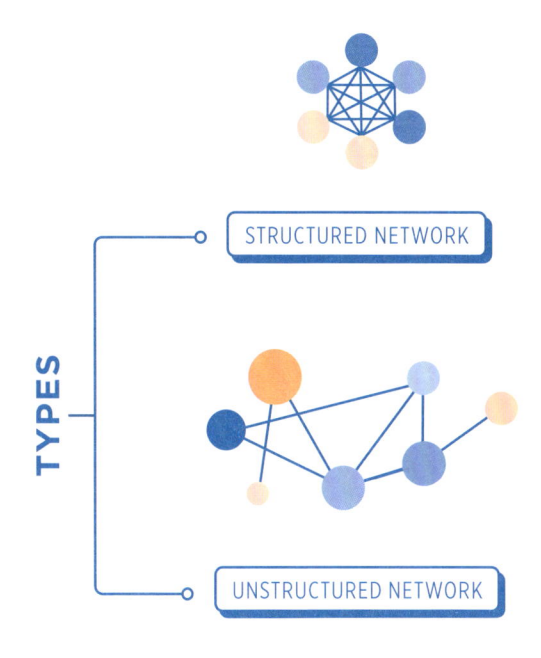

Structured Network: Although the network is decentralised, it has a high degree of formality and rules.

Unstructured Network: A Value Network with little formality or formal rules.

It is key to understand how your IVN is currently functioning and then make decisions on what type of structure you will need for effective scaling. You may find that there is a combination of the IVN models or a hybrid model. What is important is to understand how it is structured and managed, and to ensure that this enables the Inner Value Network to function as you have envisaged it in steps 2 and 3. Each type of IVN structure will require different types of partnering arrangement and agreements.

EXERCISE › MAPPING YOUR INNER VALUE NETWORK

Go back to your Value Network Map (→ p. 219), identifying each node and how they are connected to your organisation and each other. It can also be useful to use the size of each node to denote how much power they have in the Value Network.

Monitoring your OVN

For entities in the Outer Value Network, if you are not planning to bring them into your IVN during the next phase of the journey, you will still need to monitor them. Indeed, for entities such as cartographers, you may even want to influence them through lobbying or advocacy to ensure that they are setting the boundaries in a way that maximises value. We recommend that you regularly carry out the following actions when it comes to monitoring your OVN.

COMPETITORS: Regularly carry out assessments on their offerings to ensure that you are still adding more value than they are. Be particularly mindful of new competitors, scanning for them across the different types of competition outlined in Chapter IV. Remember, most disruption comes from new competitors entering the market in a way that the incumbents dismiss as they are targeting less profitable/valuable Value Consumers. These new entrants may well come from the Movers category, so ensure you are up to date with any potential challenges coming from that category.

CARTOGRAPHERS: Be aware of new policies, regulations and laws that are being discussed and debated. Identify policy windows and forums where you can try to influence changes to maximise the value created in the Value Network. Look for partners who you could collaborate with to advocate for change. Ensure that you understand the cartographers in each new market or territory that you are entering; they may not just be formal, but also informal power holders such as community gatekeepers. Remember that cartographers can play a big role in creating barriers to entry that can hinder you.

COMPLEMENTORS: Ensure you are clear on understanding the changes in complementors. These could be technological; they could also be new complementors emerging or previously reliable ones discontinuing. Do those complementors exist in the new markets or territories you are trying to scale into? It may well be that complementors are turning into competitors. Ensure you regularly monitor your complementors to see if these types of changes are happening and analyse what the impacts could be for you. «

CHAPTER XIII — SUMMARY
WHAT YOU HAVE LEARNED IN THIS CHAPTER

▷ How to **identify** entities playing value roles in your Value Network.

▷ The way to **visualise** your Value Network on the Value Network map.

▷ Applying a structured approach to Value Network **action planning**.

▷ Ways to construct and **manage** your Inner Value Network and what to **monitor** in your Outer Value Network.

CHAP XIV
SCALE STRATEGY

This chapter draws together the different information you have been collecting as you work through the execution part of this book. It provides a way to use this information to develop a concise Scale Strategy Map.

YOUR SCALE STRATEGY

You are now in a position to articulate a high-level scale strategy to get you to your scale goal. This is done by pulling together the work you have carried out in the previous chapters. The strategy is to get you from your base camp, across the chasm, all the way to your first camp (your scale goal).

Imagine that in order to get there you need to cross the chasm on a wooden plank bridge suspended by rope. You can see the bridge and you can see that nearly all of the planks are in place. Each plank represents a tactic that we have outlined in this book. The issue you face is that for your own innovation or enterprise you are not sure which planks will actually hold you. So, as you cross the bridge, you need to test each plank first before fully committing to it. You will need to do this through experimentation and testing.

SETTING YOUR SCALE STRATEGY FROM BASE CAMP

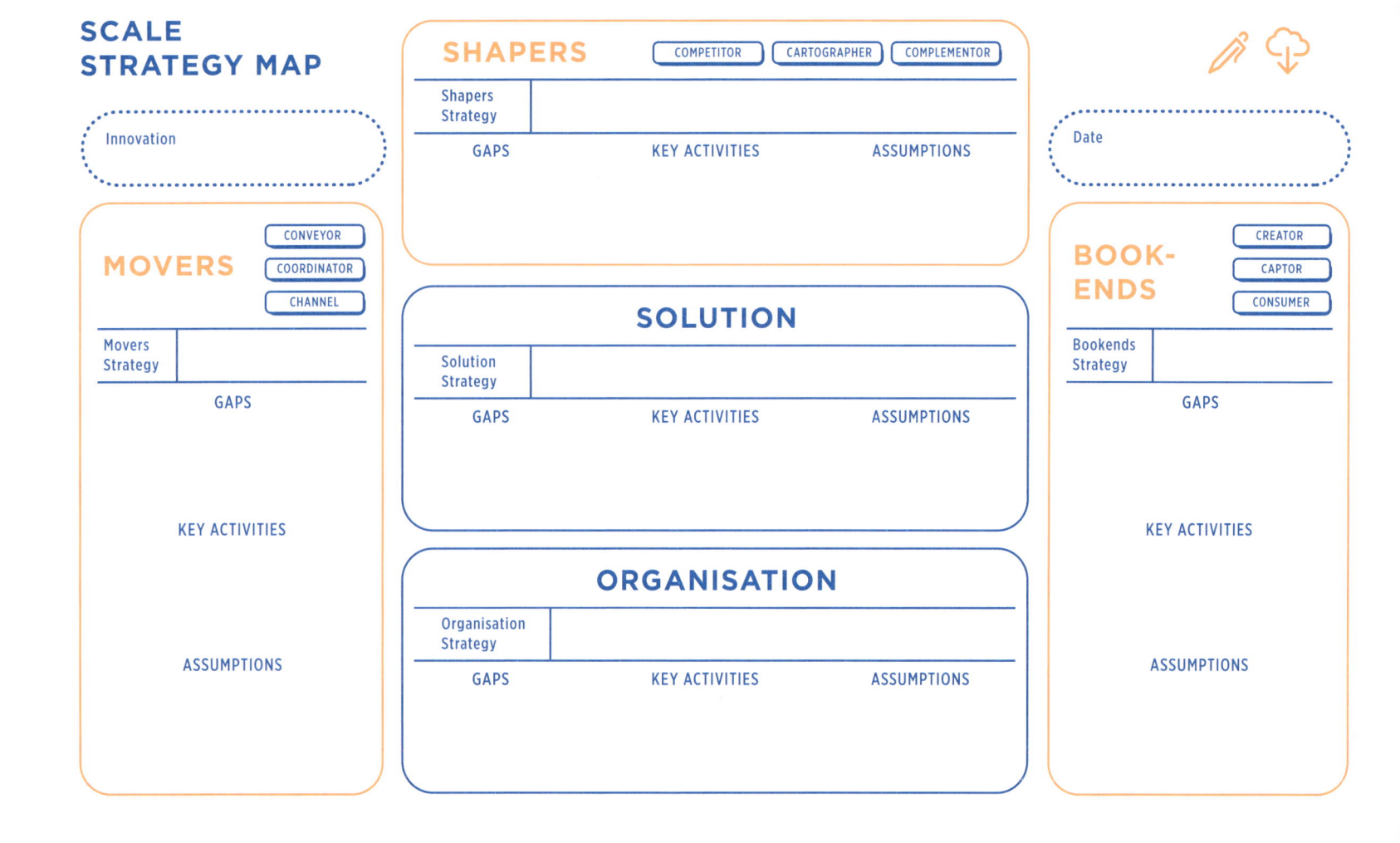

SCALE STRATEGY MAP

PART 2 — WORKING ON YOUR JOURNEY TO SCALE

Innovation

Date

SHAPERS
- COMPETITOR
- CARTOGRAPHER
- COMPLEMENTOR

Shapers Strategy

GAPS — KEY ACTIVITIES — ASSUMPTIONS

MOVERS
- CONVEYOR
- COORDINATOR
- CHANNEL

Movers Strategy

GAPS

KEY ACTIVITIES

ASSUMPTIONS

SOLUTION

Solution Strategy

GAPS — KEY ACTIVITIES — ASSUMPTIONS

ORGANISATION

Organisation Strategy

GAPS — KEY ACTIVITIES — ASSUMPTIONS

BOOK-ENDS
- CREATOR
- CAPTOR
- CONSUMER

Bookends Strategy

GAPS

KEY ACTIVITIES

ASSUMPTIONS

We do this by first creating a Scale Strategy Map. This map will show what your strategy is for each of the areas we have covered in this book: Solution, Organisation and Value Network (Bookends, Movers and Shapers). You will then outline where the key gaps are for each area are, what your tactics are to bridge those gaps, and finally what assumptions you are making.

First print out the largest version of the *Scale Strategy Map* you can.

Step 1 — Prioritise Gaps

Go back through the book and identify where the key gaps are in the scale assessment at the end of each relevant chapter. Prioritise the ones that are most critical for you to address in order to reach your scale goal. Place each one on a sticky note in the gap areas under the relevant area (e.g., a critical gap from the organisation chapter would be placed under the critical gap heading in the organisation box of the Scale Strategy Map).

Step 2 — Tactics

Identify tactics to address each of the gaps you have put on your Scale Strategy Map. They could be exercises that we have outlined in this book, such as codification of your innovation or mapping your organisational culture. It may be work that needs to be done that we have not covered in this book and you have captured in the 'other gaps' sections of the end-of-chapter scale assessments. Each of these tactics are a plank of your scale bridge and will make up your top-level work plan for the journey to scale.

As stated above, you will need to test each of these tactics before fully committing to them. Experiment, test, learn, iterate and then proceed with confidence.

Step 3 — Assumptions

Even before you start testing your strategies, you need to uncover what assumptions you may be making about your gaps and tactics. So, list your assumptions for each of the tactics and gaps and then capture the most important assumptions. These are the ones that if you are wrong about them, the strategy for addressing the gap will not work.

Assumptions can be either tested or tracked. If an assumption is within your sphere of control, you should turn it into a hypothesis and create a test for it. If the assumption is way outside your sphere of control, such as a growing economy in the market you are scaling into, then you can only track it.

For the 🔗 ASSUMPTIONS that are testable, create tests for each one and test as many as you can before you embark on your strategies.

Step 4 — Strategy One-Liners

Review your gaps, tactics and assumptions for each area and sum them up with a short one-line description of the strategy e.g., under Movers you could say, 'switch channel from retail outlets to selling direct to consumers over the internet'.

ASSUMPTIONS TRACKING AND TESTING

Follow this QR code for a handy tool for tracking and testing assumptions.

CHAPTER XIV — SUMMARY
WHAT YOU HAVE LEARNED IN THIS BOOK

If you have worked your way through this book, you now have all the key ingredients for a successful scaling journey. You have:

▷ Your scale panorama, including your scale vision, your scale route, scale goal and an outline of the barriers and critical success factors for making the climb.

▷ Your Value Network map, value role action board and Inner Value Network management approach.

▷ Your Scale Strategy Map for getting to your scale goal.

Pull them all together and check that they are coherent and make sense. You can use these as the maps and charts for your scaling journey. Remember that the terrain and weather might change dramatically as you are on the climb, so always use an iterative approach to testing your assumptions and implementing your strategies. Changing your route when you are on the climb is not a failure; it is often key to ultimate success.

BON VOYAGE
JOHN AND IAN

AFTERWORD

LOOKING ACROSS THE RANGE

We've covered a lot of ground in this book. We hope that it helps you understand the challenge of scale but also to feel confident that there is a map for the expedition and plenty of tools, techniques and accumulated experience to help you make your own journey.

Inevitably we've had to simplify some themes and leave other questions unexplored. It's a bit like standing on the top of our current mountain summit and looking across to other peaks in the range. There's always more we could cover.

In particular there's a lot more to explore around these themes and we've put some signposts in to help you if you'd like to explore them further.

The additional challenges in social innovation where assembling the ecosystem might involve many different players with very different agendas and priorities – like governments, NGOs, donor agencies, commercial businesses and aid workers.

The difficulty or working in complex multilayer markets (like healthcare or humanitarian aid) where the 'buyers' may not be the end users.

The challenge of 'dominant designs' – innovation trajectories are not always established around the 'best' innovation but rather the best fit with competing technologies and market expectations. But once dominant designs become established it's very hard to change them – like swimming upstream against the current.

At the extreme, the innovation we might wish to introduce and scale may represent a direct challenge to the established order – it is a 'disruptive' innovation. What we've learned about this kind of transition is that it involves moving aside an existing Value Network and replacing it with a new one, often with very different constituents. We hope to come back with more guidance on these particular challenges in our next book.

Stay tuned!

FURTHER RESOURCES

HERE ARE A NUMBER OF MORE DETAILED AND RESEARCH-BASED RESOURCES WHICH COVER THE FIELD OF SCALING INNOVATION

Everett Rogers's pioneering work on diffusion of innovation provides a very detailed synthesis of influential factors in scaling **[1]**

Geoffrey Moore coined the term 'crossing the chasm' in his book of the same name which explores the challenge of getting early adopters on board to help accelerate scaling **[2]**

David Albury's work for the UK Cabinet Office **[3]** and the Health Foundation **[4]** reviews in depth the challenges of scaling innovations in a multi-layered market: healthcare in the UK

ELRHA have published several reports including an overview of the scaling challenge **[5]** and detailed reports on themes like the role of evidence **[6]** and the challenge of ecosystem development

NESTA's **'Making It Big'** report **[7]** provides an overview of their extensive work on scaling social innovation

IDIA – the **International Development Innovation Alliance** – have a very useful report distilling experience across their membership in the area of scaling social innovation **[8]**

The **World Food Programme** has invested heavily in innovation accelerators including some support for scaling innovations to impact. They have a valuable library of resources here which capture that experience. › *https://innovation.wfp.org/what-we-do*

UNICEF has worked extensively in the area of **innovation support** and has accumulated considerable useful experience around scaling, the key insights being contained in this report.
› *https://www.unicef.org/innovation/sites/unicef.org.innovation/files/2019-03/Scaling Innovation For Every Child_0.pdf*

CAP-Gemini carried out a widespread consultative review on the scaling challenge and their report is here **[9]**

Frank Mattes has a useful book looking at the challenges of scaling inside larger organisations **[9]**

The challenge of **complementary assets** is explored well in the work of David Teece **[10]**

And Teece's work also covers the issue of **'appropriability regimes'** in the context of scaling innovation **[11]**

Further exploration on the challenge of **organizational culture** can be found in this essential strategy text **[12]**

[1] Rogers, E. (2003). *Diffusion of innovations* (5th ed.). Free Press.

[2] Moore, G. (1999). *Crossing the chasm – Marketing and selling high-techproducts to mainstream customers.* Harper Business.

[3] Albury, D. (2004). *Innovation in the public sector* Strategy Unit, Cabinet Office, London, Working paper.

[4] Albury, D. (2018). *Against the odds: Successfully scaling innovations in the NHS.* The Health Foundation, London.

[5] Gray, I. and McClure, D. (2018). *Too tough to scale.* ELRHA, London.

[6] Dodgson, K. (2021). *Using evidence to drive the adoption of humanitarian Innovations.* ELRHA, London.

[7] NESTA (2014). *Making it big.* NESTA, London.

[8] IDIA (2017). *Scaling innovations.* International Development Innovation Alliance.

[9] Mattes, F. (2021). *Lean scale-up.* Innovation 3G.

[10] Teece, D. (1998). Capturing value from knowledge assets: The new economy, markets for know-how, and intangible assets. *California management review,* 40 (3), Article 3.

[11] Teece, D. (1986). Profiting from technological innovation: Implications for integration, collaboration, licensing and public policy. *Research policy*, 15: 285 – 305.

[12] Johnson, G., Scholes, K. & Whittington, R. (2008). *Exploring corporate strategy,* 8th edition, Harlow et al.: Pearson Education Limited.

ACKNOWLEDGE-MENTS

As we've said often in this book, innovation is a multiplayer game and we've benefitted from many people's support and encouragement in this project. Particular thanks on my side go to friends and colleagues at the Universities of Exeter and Stavanger where I've explored many of the ideas in the book and to others in the many organisations with whom I've worked in both public and private sector in trying to understand the journey to scale.

As always I owe a big debt to my wife Anna for her support and my daughter Lara for her patience in waiting for me to finish writing before we could do useful stuff like playing!

And of course both Ian and I would like to thank Steve, Lucy, André and the rest of the team at De Gruyter and Editienne for their help in realising this innovation project.

JOHN BESSANT

Just as you need a team to help you climb mount scale, I have benefited from working with a Value Network of collaborators on my journey to understanding scale.

First of all, I want to thank all of the leaders, teams and organisations I have had the pleasure to mentor on their scaling journeys over the past decade. You are too many to mention, but you have each provided me with insights and inspiration from your own scaling journeys. For those organisations that have commissioned me and my team to run your scale accelerators. Thank you. I have appreciated the chance to trial and test all the tools we have created with you. There have been some particularly close climbers over the years, and I want to highlight the contribution of Dan McClure who I first got into exploring this field with in our early research and paper on the 'missing middle', and Michelle Halse for collaborating on our innovation partnerships course which helped stress test the value roles and typologies.

Closer to home, I want to say thanks to my parents for the immense support they have provided over the years. You have both gone above and beyond, and I truly appreciate it. For Anya and Keziah, thanks for your patience as your Dad has worked long hours and travelled incessantly. I could not have asked for two more amazing daughters. Madara, thankyou for our life in technicolour! Thanks for encouraging me and pushing me when I needed it. You are one in a billion.

IAN GRAY

ABOUT THE AUTHORS

STAY IN TOUCH
info@scalingvalue.org

IAN GRAY

is a seasoned strategist, innovator, and partnership expert with 25 years of experience in driving transformative change. As the Founder of Gray Dot Catalyst, he has guided over 100 organizations, businesses, and innovations on their journeys of growth and success through his accelerator programs, mentoring, advising, and training initiatives.

Ian's expertise spans diverse industries and geographies; his work has taken him from London to Nairobi, San Francisco to Chennai, Sydney to Goma, Geneva to Lima, and many places in between. He is a patented inventor and holds an M.A. (Hons), MSc (Econ), and MBA. His real passion lies in supporting disruptive innovations that address critical global challenges.

Find out more about Ian's work on:

Innovation Scaling

Innovation Partnerships

Strategy

JOHN BESSANT

STAY IN TOUCH
info@scalingvalue.org

Originally a chemical engineer, John Bessant has been active in the field of research and consultancy in technology and innovation management for over 40 years. He is Emeritus Professor of Innovation and Entrepreneurship at the University of Exeter, United Kingdom and also has visiting appointments at the University of Stavanger, Norway and the University of Erlangen-Nuremberg, Germany.

He has acted as advisor to various national governments, to international bodies including the United Nations, the World Bank and the OECD and to a wide range of companies. He is the author of over 40 books and monographs and many articles on the topic of innovation management; the most recent include *Managing Innovation* (2020) (now in its 7th edition), *Entrepreneurship* (2018) and Riding the Innovation Wave (2017). You can find more and follow his blog at www.johnbessant.org.

ISBN 978-3-11-078947-8
e-ISBN (PDF) 978-3-11-078981-2
ISSN 2940-2360

Library of Congress Control Number: 2023938429

Bibliographic information published by the Deutsche Nationalbibliothek
The Deutsche Nationalbibliothek lists this publication in the Deutsche
Nationalbibliografie; detailed bibliographic data are available on the internet
at http://dnb.dnb.de.

© 2024 Walter de Gruyter GmbH, Berlin/Boston
Design, Illustration and Typesetting: Editienne, Berlin
Printing and Binding: optimal media GmbH, Röbel

www.degruyter.com